MALIK GOES TO SCHOOL

*Examining the Language Skills
of African American Students
From Preschool–5th Grade*

MALIK GOES TO SCHOOL

Examining the Language Skills
of African American Students
From Preschool–5th Grade

Holly K. Craig
University of Michigan

Julie A. Washington
Wayne State University

LEA   LAWRENCE ERLBAUM ASSOCIATES, PUBLISHERS
2006   Mahwah, New Jersey   London

Lawrence Erlbaum Associates, Inc., Publishers
10 Industrial Avenue
Mahwah, New Jersey 07430
www.erlbaum.com

Cover design by Kathryn Houghtaling Lacey

Library of Congress Cataloging-in-Publication Data

Craig, Holly K.
  Malik goes to school : examining the language skills of African American students from
preschool–5th grade / Holly K. Craig, Julie A. Washington.
    p. cm.
  Includes bibliographical references and index.
  ISBN 0-8058-4089-3 (cloth : alk. paper)
  ISBN 0-8058-5811-3 (pbk. : alk. paper)
  1. African American children—Language. 2. African American children—Education.
3. Language arts—United States. 4. Black English. I. Washington, Julie A. II. Title.

PE3102.N42C73 2005
427′.973′08996073—dc22   2005040132
                                                                                  CIP

Printed in the United States of America
10 9 8 7 6 5 4 3 2 1

*This book is dedicated to
Jerry, Darryl, Justin, and Miles,
and to all the students, their families,
and teachers who have worked with
us over the past 10 years.*

CONTENTS

FOREWORD

Walt Wolfram
North Carolina State University

In an important sense, this book encapsulates the evolution of research studies on African American English (AAE) over the past half-century. It is safe to say that no variety of English has been more described and debated in the history of sociolinguistics, with an unrelenting proliferation of literature. But this is not just another book in the series of publications. Holly Craig and Julie Washington have managed to accomplish what few of their predecessors have achieved—offered a set of best practices for applying information about AAE based on a comprehensive research program. Only a substantive research agenda carried out with large numbers of AAE speakers over an extended period of time could earn someone the right to make the kinds of recommendations set forth here. Craig and Washington have earned that right.

Research on AAE has taken a stimulating academic journey, with intriguing speculations about its origin; reconstructions of its past and present trajectory of change; descriptions of its current linguistic status; and explanations of its sociolinguistic role in American society. Its place as a primary subfield of sociolinguistics is secure. But it is also now time to pause and to reflect on what has been accomplished—especially with respect to the motivations that sparked the original interest and ignited the extended inquiry. The earliest studies of AAE, conducted many names ago (Negro Dialect, Nonstandard Negro English, Black English, Black English Vernacular, Ebonics, among others), were funded largely by federal educational and social agencies inspired by President Lyndon B. Johnson's "War on Poverty" set in motion in 1964. Among other dimensions of poverty, it was observed that poor children, including many African Americans, showed an alarming gap in their educational achievement compared to their middle-class White peers—the so-called "Black–White achievement gap." The correlation between the use of a vernacular dialect and educational failure seemed to be fairly transparent, but how might the linguistic differences factor into the educational disparity? Decades later, we are still in the process of answering this question, but this study brings us one step closer.

The persistence of some of the fundamental issues related to language difference and educational achievement has been frustrating at times, but it is also important to acknowledge that substantial progress has taken place over this period. First of all, there has been a change in PERSPECTIVE AND POL-ICY related to language diversity in general and AAE in particular. Just a few decades ago, the distinct linguistic features of African American English were not differentiated from language disorders, and no accommodation of systematic dialect differences was admitted in assessment and achievement. In fact, my own interest in the application of sociolinguistics to assessment was piqued originally by a survey of young school children in Washington, D.C., in the mid-1960s, which showed that more than half of the students entering the public school system indicated significant speech and language delays (Hurst, 1965). It was hardly a coincidence that the population of students enrolled in the school system at the time was overwhelmingly African American, the majority of whom spoke a vernacular variety of AAE. Such reports, fueled by educational psychologists who observed that Black children of poverty were typically a couple of years behind their middle-class White peers in their language development (Bereiter & Englemann, 1966), inspired the difference–deficit debates of the 1960s. To their credit, prominent national professional organizations such as the American Speech-Language-Hearing Association (ASHA) and the National Council of Teachers of English (NCTE) wrestled with the issue of difference versus deficit, and revised their policies related to language differences. For example, both ASHA (Position Statement on Social Dialects, 1983) and NCTE (Committee on College Composition and Communication Language Statement, 1974) adopted strong position statements supporting the linguistic integrity of all varieties of English regardless of their social valuation. In fact, I have sometimes observed that no professional national organization has shown more progress than ASHA in changing its viewpoint on language diversity. Admittedly, the application of these policies on a grass-roots level still lags, but there is no question that institutional perspectives and policies have been transformed.

There has also been a proliferation of DESCRIPTIVE DETAIL with respect to the linguistic traits of AAE. The earliest studies of AAE structures (e.g., Fasold, 1972; Fasold & Wolfram, 1970; Labov, Cohen, Robbins, & Lewis, 1968; Wolfram, 1969) set forth many of the major phonological and grammatical traits used by adolescent and adult speakers of AAE in large metropolitan areas of the North. From that point, studies of AAE expanded in several ways. Descriptive studies have extended to the Southern, rural linguistic roots of AAE so that we now know more about the regional context of this variety—or more properly, the varieties of AAE. Descriptive studies further uncovered structures not included in the earlier descriptions. In some cases these structures were simply overlooked or "camouflaged" in earlier studies while other structures represent more recent innovations. As any language variety, AAE is dynamic rather than static, and it is constantly undergoing change. In the early days of our descriptive studies of AAE (Fasold & Wolfram 1970), for example, we were intrigued with the creole-like use of *say* to introduce a quote as in *She tell him, say, "Why you here?"*; today, we are impressed with how widespread the use of quotative *like* (e.g., *She like, "Why you here?"*) has become among younger AAE speakers over a compressed timeframe—in ways that parallel its use in most mainstream varieties of American English (Cukor-Avila, 2002). Studies have also expanded to include pragmatic and discourse traits found in African American English to complement the phonological and grammatical details that preoccupied most early linguistic studies. And research now includes a wider age range of speakers, including dedicated research on the developmental acquisition of AAE. Descriptive structural accounts of AAE as well as analyses of the variable use of AAE structures are now readily available in the sociolinguistic literature, as demonstrated in the appendix of structures used in the various analyses reported in this book.

There has also been significant advancement in the APPLICATION OF SOCIO-LINGUISTIC KNOWLEDGE in fields that range from developmental evaluation to literacy. This application is modeled well in the chapters of this book for children K through Grade 5, the critical stage of early education. More than three decades ago, in 1972, my colleagues Orlando Taylor, Ronald Williams, and I conducted a symposium at an annual ASHA convention in which we predicted, based on contrastive linguistic analysis, dialect-appropriate, alternative responses for AAE speakers that could be applied to some of the most commonly used standardized testing instruments used by speech and language pathologists at the time. Our concern was motivated by the fact that the standardized testing instruments did not acknowledge the possibility of dialect responses that might constitute legitimate, alternative norms for speakers from dialects other than Standard American English. Although this concern has not subsided, the recognition of alternative dialect options has become a reality, thanks in part to research efforts of Holly Craig, Julie Washington, and their colleagues. It has even led to the development of new testing instruments specifically designed to include AAE dialect variation, such as the Diagnostic Evaluation of Language Variation (Seymour, Roeper, & de Villiers, 2003). Though we still may not be satisfied that a full battery of dialect-fair assessment instruments is now available to speech and language diagnosticians, we must certainly acknowledge the increased sensitivity to language variation. A couple of decades ago, the battery of instruments that comprises the *Michigan Protocol for African American Language* (see chapter 7) would not have been possible. Testing instruments in speech and language development can no longer ignore the issue of dialect differences in assessment, though they may deal with them in a variety of ways—from supplementary lists of appropriate responses for speakers of AAE and other vernacular varieties to a focus on more universal levels of language organization that are not as prone to dialect differences as are the superficial levels of phonology and morphosyntax. Given the inescapable grip that testing holds on our society and the increasing reliance on "bottom-line" test scores for measuring student achievement, the challenge to provide a full complement of dialect-appropriate tests for AAE speakers remains critical. The level of dialect awareness, research, and application represented in the chapters of this book is indeed most welcome.

Finally, there is the issue of DIALECT ENLIGHTENMENT. In many respects, the greatest obstacle faced by speakers of AAE remains the socialized attitudes that the American public holds about language differences. Ultimately, language ideology, the assumed set of beliefs about the way language is and the way it should be, provides the foundational basis for the institutionalized ways that AAE and its speakers have been treated in our society. Furthermore, it must be recognized that language conflicts are not ultimately about language per se, but the power of language to serve as a proxy for broader sociopolitical and cultural issues. The transparency of language as cultural behavior makes it an ideal stage for acting out much more fundamental issues and conflicts among different groups in society.

There remains a constant need for language awareness programs in a broadly based context. By language awareness here, I mean programs that are directed toward raising sensitivity to and conscious awareness of the nature of language and its role in human life. Such programs may focus on a cognitive parameter, in which the focus is on understanding the patterns of language; an affective parameter, in which the focus is on attitudes about language; or a social parameter, in which the focus is on the use of language in effective communication and interaction. Are educators, speech and language pathologists, other practitioners, and the general public aware of the nature of AAE as a linguistic system and its implications for the social and educational lives of African Americans? Certainly, more universities offer courses devoted to African American language or include information about AAE as a part of general language education, but is this sufficient? And does it make a difference? The public outcry over AAE associated with the so-called Oakland Ebonics controversy that took place in 1996–1997 suggests that sociolinguistic efforts to raise awareness about the naturalness of language differences have fallen far short of the mark. After a half-century of sociolinguistic description and application, the most pervasive and persistent challenge today continues to be the widespread application of the *principle of linguistic subordination* (Lippi-Green, 1997), in which vernacular dialects are viewed as little more than unworthy, illegitimate versions of the dominant language variety—Standard American English. The social and educational misunderstanding of the nature of language differences still qualifies as one of the great scientific myths of modern society. Beliefs about language differences are part of our primitive belief system—the same system responsible for our religious and political beliefs—so it should not surprise us that misguided beliefs about AAE have proven to be so resilient.

These beliefs are not abstract notions removed from everyday encounters. They crop up regularly in ordinary events. I recently met with a new school administrator in a public school where we had been teaching students about dialect differences for more than a decade. Although the administrator was enthusiastic about our language curriculum, one of the first questions was, "This isn't about Ebonics, is it?" This remark was clearly not intended to be a literal question about subject content, but an indirect condemnation of any educational program that might acknowledge the legitimacy of AAE. Several decades of description, application, and education, unfortunately, have had minimal impact on the public perception of AAE. There is no established tradition for public education about language awareness in American society or in our schools; it simply does not fit within current paradigms of formal and informal public education. The need for widespread information about language differences thus remains as critical today as it was a half-century ago, notwithstanding some of the noteworthy educational efforts that universities and professional organizations have made to change this tradition. While winning some important battles, we are still losing the sociolinguistic war.

The research results and application paradigm presented by Craig and Washington need to be confronted honestly by all of us who deal directly or indirectly with AAE speakers. The results of their studies are cause for alarm at the slow pace of progress, but they also offer hope. The infamous Black–White achievement gap is still here—a sobering fact that should be of concern to all of us. At the same time, Craig's and Washington's grounded research and judicious recommendations offer guidelines for those who wish to translate good intentions into the equitable treatment of AAE speakers.

As we consider their research and recommendations, it is important to realize that Craig and Washington offer more than an accumulated set of impersonal facts and figures. These are real faces telling personal stories. They are the stories of Malik and other children who have been the victims of sociolinguistic abuse and discrimination. They are the stories of educators and diagnosticians who have deliberately or unwittingly failed to take language differences into consideration in their treatment of vernacular dialect speakers. And they are the hurtful stories of our friends and acquaintances who still have nothing but contempt and condemnation for the heritage language variety that represents the African American cultural experience. While affirming our progress, this book should inspire us to do more—and to do it better. The stakes are simply too high to do otherwise.

REFERENCES

American Speech-Language-Hearing Association (1983). Position statement on social dialects. *Asha, 25*(9), 24.

Bereiter, C., & Englemann, S. (1966). *Teaching disadvantaged children in the preschool.* Englewood Cliffs, NJ: Prentice-Hall.

Committee on CCC Language Statement (1974). Students' rights to their own language. *College Composition and Communication* 25 (special issue). Champaign-Urbana, IL: National Council of Teachers of English.

Cukor-Avila, P. (2002). *She say, she go, she be like:* Verbs of quotation over time in African American Vernacular English. *American Speech, 77,* 3–31.

Fasold, R. W. (1972). *Tense marking in Black English.* Washington, DC: Center for Applied Linguistics.

Fasold, R. W., & Wolfram, W. (1970). Some linguistic features of Negro dialect. In R. W. Fasold & R. W. Shuy (Eds.), *Teaching standard English in the inner city, Volume 6* (pp. 41–86). Washington, DC: Center for Applied Linguistics.

Hurst, C. G. (1965). *Psychological correlates of dialectolalia.* Washington, DC: Howard University.

Labov, W., Cohen, P., Robins, C., & Lewis, J. (1968). *A study of the Non-Standard English of Negro and Puerto Rican Speakers in New York City.* Cooperative Research Project No. 3288. Washington, DC: Cooperative Research Program of the Office of Education, U.S. Department of Health, Education, and Welfare.

Lippi-Green, R. (1997). *English with an accent: Language, ideology, and discrimination in the United States.* London: Routledge.

Seymour, H. N., Roeper, T., & de Villiers, J. (1999). *Diagnostic Evaluation of Language Variation.* San Antonio, TX: Psychological Corporation.

Wolfram, W. (1969). *Sociolinguistic description of Detroit Negro Speech.* Washington, DC: Center for Applied Linguistics.

PREFACE

The aim of this book is to provide practicing professionals in speech–language pathology and education a summary of the work generated by our research program at the University of Michigan since the mid 1990s. This program of research focuses on the language skills of African American children in the elementary grades. The concept for the resulting monograph originated as a response to the many individuals who have attended workshops and meetings we have led and have requested a synthesis of our findings, including an integration of this information into the broader practical contexts of academic planning and clinical decision-making.

Most African American children are speakers of African American English (AAE), known variously as African American Vernacular English, Black English, or the highly politicized term *Ebonics*. Early in our research program, we discovered that what was known about AAE was derived almost exclusively from the study of older adolescents and adults during the 1960s and 1970s when the sociopolitical imperative was to determine that the language differences were systematic, culturally accepted, and not an inferior form of Standard American English. Having established the rule-governed nature of AAE, little subsequent attention was directed to its role in child development. Our first published articles, therefore, described AAE at the time of school entry, and we have since characterized important influences on the child's use of AAE. In addition, we have characterized other non-dialectal aspects of language development, those that are not feature based, in the early school years, and have contributed measures to a culture-fair, child-centered assessment protocol.

Our work to date has been published almost exclusively in the form of journal articles. This book, therefore, provides us with a vehicle to reach a wider audience than just journal readers. We relish this opportunity to integrate information across articles, and to discuss the import of our findings on a larger scale. We offer case examples, especially that of Malik, as appropriate throughout the book to illustrate many of the language and literacy findings. In addition, we discuss implications of our work for practicing professionals and readers new to the study of African American children.

Organizationally, the book provides a discussion of our major findings, and then a translation of this information into practice. The first chapter introduces Malik and situates our interest in the issue of underachievement by African American students. Chapter 2 provides a brief look at the other major lines of research in child language that address African American students, and the reader is encouraged to study the work of these scholars. Chapter 3 discusses our participant sample and the major methods used to study the language of African American students in the elementary grades. Chapters 4 and 5 detail our findings for child AAE both in terms of the features used by our student sample and major sources of variation in the production of features. In Chapter 6, we add to the characterization of the oral language skills of typically developing African American students by summarizing our findings relative to selected nondialectal aspects of their oral language. Building on the information provided in chapter 6, chapter 7 outlines a language evaluation process appropriate for the language skills of African American students. Chapters 8 and 9 discuss the academic underachievement faced by many African American students and the important contribution that oral language makes to literacy acquisition. The final chapter summarizes what we have learned to date about students like Malik. The chapters are supplemented by detailed appendixes, which provide the reader with additional discussion of particular methods.

Our goal in writing these 10 chapters has been to synthesize and interpret a decade's worth of data from our research program, thereby contextualizing it and making it accessible to a broad group of individuals interested in the welfare of African American children. We hope that students in speech–language pathology, early career teachers, or professionals new to the issues involved in the Black–White Achievement Gap will find this book informative and of practical utility to them.

ACKNOWLEDGMENTS

This book is a monograph based on a decade-long research program at the University of Michigan. We are indebted to many individuals for their contributions to the program of research, the stimulation and development of ideas, and the preparation of this volume. These include: Carol M. Connor and Connie A. Thompson, who were doctoral students, and Shurita Thomas-Tate, who was a post-doctoral fellow. They were active collaborators in many of the studies that laid the foundation for this book. Stephanie (Potter) Hensel and Erin J. Quinn provided expert data reduction and manuscript preparation, and Mary Packard oversaw data collection on many projects for many years. Many children, parents, teachers, and administrators were generous with their time and enthusiasm for our work. We acknowledge their participation with deepest gratitude.

The program of research has been funded by: National Institutes of Health, National Institute on Deafness and Other Communication Disorders, Grant 1 RO1 DC 02313-01A1, and Grant 1 RO1 DC 04273-01; the U.S. Department of Education, Office of Educational Research and Improvement, Grant R305T990368, and Grant R305R70004, and the Office of the Vice-President for Research at the University of Michigan.

—Holly K. Craig
—Julie A. Washington

1

WHO IS MALIK?[1]

Malik is an excellent example of the many African American students who are not successful academically. We first met Malik when he was a preschooler. Malik is African American and a speaker of African American English (AAE). This book is about the language of African American students, and thus about Malik and all the other school-aged African American children we have met, studied, enjoyed, and worried about over the last decade.

Malik resided in a low-income home in an urban-fringe community in the Metropolitan Detroit area. He lived with his mother, a single parent who worked as a blue collar civil servant. His family had lived in Michigan for three generations. Like most 4-year-olds, when we met Malik he was an energetic and enthusiastic child, and thoroughly enjoyed his interactions with our adult examiners.

Like other African American students, Malik's performances on all of our oral language measures showed growth across grades. As a preschooler, Malik's general cognitive abilities were average (Standard Score of 10 compared to Mean Standard Score of 10) as measured by the Triangles subtest of the Kaufman Assessment Battery for Children (K-ABC, Kaufman & Kaufman, 1983). Malik's use of AAE was measured with a Dialect Density Measure (DDM), calculated as the rate of feature production per words (Craig, Washington, & Thompson-Porter, 1998a). He was a speaker of AAE, and was a moderate to heavy dialect user (see chapter 5 for more detail on ranges of DDMs). In contrast to most of his peers, across grades he showed no evi-

---

[1]Although Malik represents a real child this was not his name. His name was changed to preserve confidentiality.

dence of dialect shifting toward SAE (see chapter 5). Rather, his use of dialect appeared to increase over time (see Table 1.1).

All classrooms are language based. Oral language skills provide the foundation for the development of reading and writing (Catts, 1991; Catts, Fey, Zhang, & Tomblin, 1999; Snow & Tabors, 1993). Consequently, children who have difficulty acquiring spoken language skills or who speak a different variety of English other than that of the majority population are at risk for failure to acquire proficient reading skills. Many elementary-grade African American students speak AAE (Craig & Washington, 2002). AAE is a systematic, rule-governed linguistic variety of English (Baugh, 1983; Labov, 1972; Mufwene, Rickford, Bailey, & Baugh, 1998; Smitherman, 1977; Stockman, 1996; Washington & Craig, 1994; Wolfram & Fasold, 1974). AAE morpho-syntactic, phonological, lexical, prosodic, and discourse features differ considerably from Standard American English (SAE) and formal SAE, sometimes called School English (SE) or Mainstream Classroom English (MCE), is the language of the classroom and curriculum (Dillard, 1972; Hester, 1996; Labov, 1998; Morgan, 1998; Smitherman, 1998; Wolfram, 1994).

TABLE 1.1
Malik's Oral Language and Cognitive Performance
Scores at Preschool (P) and Grade 4

Measure	Actual Scores		Expected Scores	
	P	4	P	4
Triangles				
subtest of the Kaufman Assessment Battery for Children	8	10	10	10
DDM				
Dialect Density Measure calculated as a ratio of morpho-syntactic features to words	.068	.105	.108	.038
MLCU				
Mean Length of Communication Unit	4.5	5.8	4.38	7.33
Csyn				
Proportional frequencies of Complex Syntax	.25	.44	.24	.69
RevS				
Reversible Sentences task designed to probe comprehension of the active-passive voice distinction	7	13	12.0	≥ 18.5/20
PPVT–III				
Peabody Picture Vocabulary Test–3rd edition	NT*	91	100	100
Wh-q				
Frequencies of correct responses to Wh-questions	48/72	107/114	49.3	107.2

Note. *NT = Not tested. Expected fourth-grade scores from "Oral Language Expectations for African American Children in Grades 1 Through 5," by H. K. Craig, J. A. Washington, and C. A. Thompson, in press.

Like most of the typically developing African American students participating in our research program, Malik's oral language skills were within the
average range at preschool and grew somewhat as he got older. Malik's
oral language skills are summarized for preschool and fourth grade in Table
1.1. His performance on the Peabody Picture Vocabulary Test III (PPVT–III,
Dunn & Dunn, 1997) revealed borderline low average responses (Standard
Score of 91 compared to a Mean Standard Score of 100) on this receptive vocabulary test. His receptive grammar skills also seemed low average at
best, as evidenced by his failure to consistently distinguish the active-
passive sentence distinction when presented a reversible sentences task
(RevS, Craig, Washington, & Thompson-Porter, 1998b). Most students were
able to consistently comprehend active from passive syntactic sentence
structures and performed at ceiling on this task by first grade, whereas
Malik had not gained this level of understanding by fourth grade.

On other oral language measures, his performances were comparable to
his African American grade-level peers, showing increases in performance
levels across the elementary years. This included his average sentence
length, measured as Mean Length of Communication Unit (MLCU), proportional frequencies of complex syntactic structures relative to Communication
Units (Csyn), and frequencies of correct responses to increasingly challenging requests for information in the form of wh-question responses (Wh-q).
Each of these measures is discussed in more detail in chapters 6 and 7.

Like many African American students, as we followed Malik's progress
throughout the elementary grades, it became clear that his academic
achievement was low, and was declining relative to expectations with increasing grades. For reading, his Oral Reading Quotient (ORQ) from the
Gray Oral Reading Test, 3rd edition (Wiederholt & Bryant, 1992) was low average in second grade (ORQ = 91), and below average (ORQ = 85) in fourth
grade (mean ORQ = 100).

In addition, Table 1.2 presents Malik's performances on the Metropolitan
Achievement Tests (MAT, 1993), a nationally standardized achievement
test, and on the Michigan Educational Assessment Program (MEAP, 1999-
2000), a statewide criterion referenced test that is administered beginning
in fourth grade. Malik's scores on these instruments revealed poor across-
the-board performances. For example, on the reading portion of the test,
his achievement was best at first grade, but even this performance was only
at the 20th percentile. Expected performances would be around the 50th
percentile at each grade. As elementary grade levels increased, his percentile scores decreased. On the MEAP, Malik's Math score was nearly one
standard deviation below the mean and his Story and Information scores,
both measures of reading proficiency, were more than one standard deviation below the mean for the cohort of Michigan fourth graders who took the
MEAP that year.

TABLE 1.2
Malik's Scores for the MAT and the MEAP

	MAT (Percentiles)			MEAP (Scaled scores)		
Grade	Reading	Science	Math	Story	Info	Math
1	20	*	4	*	*	*
2	8	9	2	*	*	*
3	5	*	4	*	*	*
4	*	*	*	279	261	512
				M = 317	M = 303	M = 539.5
5	9	*	12	*	*	*
6	5	*	3	*	*	*

Note. * = Test/subtest not administered at these grades. Expected scores on the MAT = 50th percentile. Expected scores on the MEAP are the means (*M*) for that year.

Questionnaires tapped the classroom teacher's perceptions of Malik's abilities. At fourth grade Malik's teacher indicated that he had great difficulty expressing himself and in comprehending, but she rated reading as only of average difficulty for him. She characterized his overall classroom performance as "below average" compared to other children in his class and felt that he did not play well with other children. Her expectations were that Malik would likely complete high school but it was unlikely that he would attend college.

In contrast, at fourth grade Malik's mother felt that it was "very easy" for him to express himself and he had no difficulty comprehending. She felt that all academic areas were important, ranking reading and science as extremely important. His mother felt that Malik found all academic subjects to be easy. She was sure that he would both graduate high school and college, and rated his classroom performance overall as "average." When asked: what would you like your child to be when he grows up? She responded: "It doesn't matter as long as he gets an education." (More information about differences in student, parent, and teacher perceptions is presented in chapter 8.)

Students like Malik are the reason that we wrote this book. Improving understanding of the reasons why the educational outcomes of Malik and other young African American students are poor is the motivation that underlies our intensive program of research at the University of Michigan. We are deeply concerned that in the earliest years of this the 21st century, Malik and many of his peers are unlikely to learn to read, as well as unlikely to be highly educated or prosperous as they grow into adulthood. These same students are no better off now than if they had been growing up in the United States in the early years of the 20th century.

Like many of his African American peers around the country, Malik is struggling to learn to read. Good reading skills are foundational to learning across the academic content areas. Malik and his African American peers are part of the Black–White Achievement Gap. They perform significantly lower than majority students in reading, science, math, and geography (Braswell, Daane, & Grigg, 2003; Grigg, Daane, Jin, & Campbell, 2003; O'Sullivan, Lauko, Grigg, Qian, & Zhang, 2003; Weiss, Lutkus, Hildebrant, & Johnson, 2002). Labeled the "Black–White Test Score Gap" (Jencks & Phillips, 1998), this disparity is measurable at school entry and continues through 12th grade (Phillips, Crouse, & Ralph, 1998). Moreover, recorded as early as 1910 (Fishback & Baskin, 1991), the Black–White Achievement Gap has persistently spanned generations of U.S. students.

If Malik had been a student during the early 1900s, he would have been enrolled in a predominantly African American school, and few resources would have been available to that school. Desegregation was society's ultimate response to bridging the gap between educational opportunities afforded to mainstream versus African American students. It was believed that by allowing African American students to attend schools with their majority peers, educational opportunity and equality would result. This has not been the case.

In addition to desegregation efforts, state and federal preschool programs represent an additional response designed to bridge the gap between low-income, minority students entering school and their majority peers. At the time when we met Malik he was enrolled in a classroom in Michigan's School Readiness Program (MSRP). In an investigation of the impact of these early intervention programs on later classroom performance we found that participation in public preschool programs can succeed in equalizing the starting point for many African American children (Craig, Connor, & Washington, 2003). Unfortunately, for Malik and many others like him, enrolling in these early childhood education programs is no guarantee of later academic success.

Fifty years after the landmark *Brown v. Board of Education* (1954), African American students are no longer in "separate" schools and, African American students remain "unequal" in academic attainment and in access to high-quality educations. Twenty-five years after *Martin Luther King Junior Elementary School Children v. Ann Arbor School District Board* (1979), African American students continue to have difficulty learning to read. The latter case is more commonly referred to as the Ann Arbor Decision, or the Black English Case. The judge found that the dialect spoken by the African American students in the case constituted a barrier between the children and the teachers, because of failure of the teachers to take dialect into account when teaching the students to read SAE. This failure was found to be due to failure by the School Board to develop a program to assist the teachers, and the School Board was required to develop and file an appropriate plan of action to address this shortcoming. The students' reading problems, experienced by all African American students in the case, were found to impede their equal participation in the school's educational program. Today urban schools enroll the greatest numbers of African American students, and regrettably, despite attempts by the states to equalize funding across districts (Headlee Amendment, 1978) and to attract the best teachers, these schools continue to have the fewest resources and worst teachers (Snow, Burns, & Griffin, 1998). Lower levels of academic achievement for African American students translate into lower adult literacy levels, lower earnings, higher levels of unemployment, and higher rates of poverty (Fishback & Baskin, 1991; Jencks & Phillips, 1998; Sable, 1998). Malik is struggling, and research suggests that he is like his peers nationally. However, Malik is not a statistic; he is a child. We need to understand why the Black–White Achievement Gap is so intractable. Past explanations for the Black–White Achievement Gap have focused primarily on the role of poverty in low achievement, and the nature of early literacy learning experiences for African American students. Our research indicates that dialect has explanatory potential as well, and this is discussed in more depth in chapter 9.

Over the last decade, our program of research has contributed in substantive ways to improving current understanding of the language and literacy skills of African American students. This book is monograph like, attempting to highlight, synthesize, and consolidate our contributions to this important body of knowledge. We have written this book for teachers, practicing clinicians, and students in training to become speech–language pathologists. The research that supports our interpretive synthesis is available in journals and each issue is appropriately referenced so that the reader can pursue the details that underpin particular issues of interest.

It has been a privilege in conducting this program of research to work with a very talented, cross-racial group of staff and students. We believe that this cross-racial collaborative has strengthened the research process. African American and White researchers often faced our research agenda with different world views, cultural assumptions, and varying priorities for finding answers to the research questions posed. What every individual shared, however, was a commitment to helping all children reach their academic potential. Examining the language of African American students from preschool through fifth grade has been our tactic, and this book describes these efforts and our findings. At the University of Michigan, residing in Ann Arbor, we live less than an hour from Metropolitan Detroit. Every researcher in our program agrees that as members of a great public university and living so close to a large urban setting where large numbers of students are failing academically, that we have a special responsibility to be involved in improving understanding of the Black–White Achievement problem. As one of our team has said: How can we live so close to Detroit and not care what happens to the city's children?

This book describes our research program in terms of its participants and methods, and then organizes our findings relative to oral language and literacy outcomes. We hope that the issues raised in this book are of interest to broad segments of society. We believe that this information will prove valuable to teachers and practicing clinicians whether they have responsibility for educating one African American student like Malik, or many.

2

AN OVERVIEW OF RESEARCH ON CHILD AAE

This chapter provides a brief overview of the major lines of research focusing on African American children who speak AAE. No line of research is exclusively associated with a single scholar or language laboratory. Whereas the study of child AAE speakers is a fairly recent focus for intensive inquiry, most researchers have had to address issues framed within more than one major line of research at one time or another, as they lay the groundwork for their own research programs. This cross-fertilization of ideas, questions, and methods has led to tremendous growth in our understanding of the African American child, child AAE, and associated language and literacy relationships. Four major lines of research are apparent in the extant literature: the search for unique features, the development of an inventory of child AAE features and the distributional properties of the inventory, the development of nondiscriminatory language and literacy evaluation procedures, and understanding the challenges faced by the AAE-speaking student in academic contexts. Each of these lines of research is discussed in the following sections.

THE SEARCH FOR UNIQUE AAE FEATURES

A central focus for theoretical linguistics is the writing of a Universal Grammar (UG). The core assumption in this daunting task is that all languages of the world can be characterized by a finite set of linguistic rules, or a grammar, which can account for a hypothetically infinite sentence output. Theoretically, the grammar will specify the functions and constraints found across all languages, and will explain the occurrence (grammatical) or nonoccurrence (ungrammatical) of every feature of the grammar of every linguistic community.

One important line of research in child AAE has been to improve understanding of the features of AAE that are distinctive, and thereby contribute to the UG. Accordingly, this line of research focuses on the acquisition of unique features and reports findings in terms of the child's linguistic competence in AAE. In order to establish uniqueness to English, four types of comparisons have been adopted. Adult models are particularly informative as they represent the benchmark for a mature and competent AAE system (Seymour & Roeper, 1999; Stockman, 1996; Wyatt, 1996). Both controlled comparisons to SAE (Seymour & Seymour, 1981) and to other nonmainstream dialects (Haynes & Moran, 1989; Hinton & Pollock, 2000; Oetting & McDonald, 2001; Pollock & Berni, 1997) are critical to determining distinctiveness of the targeted AAE features within the English grammar system. Finally, comparing feature productions by typically developing African American students to those with language impairments tests the grammaticality of the hypothesized rule (Battle, 1996; Oetting, Cantrell, & Horohov, 1999; Oetting & McDonald, 2001).

The most neutral definition of the word dialect defines it simply as a language variety shared by a group of speakers (Wolfram & Schilling-Estes, 1998). Diversity in spoken dialects can be impacted by any number of important social variables, including racial and ethnic group membership. Nonstandard varieties of English such as AAE evidence predictable and systematic variations from standard varieties of English. Labov and Harris (1986) as well as others suggested that the social segregation experienced by African Americans has resulted in the divergence of AAE from standard English varieties rather than the gradual convergence expected by linguistics. Although divergence has been documented from some features of AAE (e.g., completive done) widespread divergence from SAE has not been demonstrated (Wolfram & Schilling-Estes, 1998).

Many sentences generated by AAE speakers evidence considerable overlap with SAE. For example, the heaviest feature producer in the Craig and Washington (2004a) report, a first-grade male residing in an urban, middle-income home, produced AAE variations from SAE at the rate of approximately one feature for every 2.3 words. Therefore, even for this extreme case, slightly less than half of his words varied from comparable renderings in SAE, and just over half were produced in a way that overlapped with how they would be spoken by an SAE-speaking student. Table 2.1 illustrates this point by presenting part of a picture description elicited from Malik. As can be seen from Malik's sample, two sentences included variations from SAE that were consistent with a phonological and a morpho-syntactic AAE feature (noted with *), and these features are discussed in greater depth in chapter 4. The other three sentences likely would be produced the same

TABLE 2.1
A Portion of Malik's Picture Description as a Kindergartner

Adult	Malik
tell me about this picture, Malik.	
	and they knocked the papers over.
	the car did.
	the car did it.
anything else?	
	they stopped the kids from runnin'.*
	and they came out the school.*

Note. * = sentences that include an AAE feature. Crossing Guard picture taken from Bracken Concept Development Program (Bracken, 1986).

way by an SAE-speaking student. These noncontrastive sentence structures reflect overlapping noun or verb phrase sentence constituents so that whole clauses and whole sentences do not differ from the way they would be produced in SAE. This is not to imply, however, that the African American child is shifting from SAE to AAE at the level of successive sentences. Instead, AAE is comprised of some sentence constituents that differ from SAE and some that don't. These overlapping clause and sentence level constituents are important for the development of nonbiased evaluation instruments and are discussed further in chapter 6.

In addition to noncontrastive clause and sentence constituents, Seymour, Roeper and colleagues make a further distinction between noncontrastive structures of AAE at the level of the morpho-syntactic system—the linguistic level at which most variations from SAE or "features" appear. They compare noncontrastive morpho-syntactic features to those that are contrastive as a way to search for those special features of AAE that are unique from SAE (Green, 2002; Seymour & Ralabate, 1985; Seymour & Roeper, 1999; Seymour & Seymour, 1981). For example, they consider negative concord (he don't have no friends), which communicates a single negative meaning between two negative elements within a clause, as a noncontrastive feature. Negative concord has morpho-syntactic equivalents in SAE (he doesn't have any friends, he has no friends) (Coles-White, 2004). In this sense these variations are noncontrastive, even though the forms used to express the relationship may vary between dialects. Examples of contrastive features for AAE are: aspectual "be" (she be workin'), which communicates a habitual meaning, and that has no morpho-syntactic equivalent in SAE (Green, 1998, 2000; Seymour & Roeper, 1999), and preterite "had" (and he had went to the store), which expresses simple past tense in a "had" + verb-ed syntactic slot and is used as a narrative device in AAE (Rickford & Rafal, 1996; Ross, Oetting, & Stapleton, 2004).

This line of research makes a significant theoretical contribution to the writing of a UG. It also provides strong counterevidence to lingering negative attitudes that AAE is a deficient form of SAE. A limitation of this research is the practice of using SAE as a primary standard for comparison. Unfortunately, individuals who are not schooled in linguistics can use differences from SAE to cast AAE in a negative light. Even if these studies do not adopt an AAE–SAE control group design, comparisons to SAE rules constitute de facto comparisons.

DEVELOPING THE LINGUISTIC INVENTORY OF CHILD AAE FEATURES AND DETERMINING ITS DISTRIBUTIONAL PROPERTIES

Another important line of research has been to focus on improving understanding of the student more holistically, as an AAE speaker learning in specific social-linguistic contexts. In contrast to research framed within theoretical linguistics, this research is more sociolinguistic in nature and adopts pragmatic language models and methods. The focus in this line of research is on variables that systematically affect feature production and reports findings in terms of the uses of AAE. Peer comparisons within shared linguistic communities are particularly important for interpreting these data. Unlike the search for distinctive features of AAE, comparisons to SAE are not particularly informative and avoided because comparisons of these types, relating to sociolinguistic differences between minority and majority students, have the potential to be misinterpreted. Outcomes are characterized in terms of the development of behavioral systems rather than the acquisition of features, and pragmatic competence rather than linguistic competence is the explanatory goal.

The first step in this line of research was to develop a fairly comprehensive child-based inventory of AAE features (Craig, Thompson, Washington, & Potter, 2003; Oetting & McDonald, 2001; Seymour & Ralabate, 1985; Stockman, 1996; Washington & Craig, 1994, 2002). This then permitted examination of the inventory for different rates of use relative to context, and to potentially important social-interaction variables. Important contexts for children include play and classroom activities, and AAE varies systematically on these variables (Thompson, Craig, & Washington, 2004; Washington, Craig, & Kushmaul, 1998). Social-interaction variables include social status characteristics, particularly age/grade, gender, family socioeconomic status, community type, and geographic region, and rates of AAE production again differ systematically on these variables (Craig & Washington, 2004a; Oetting et al., 1999; Oetting & Pruitt, in press; Washington & Craig, 1998). Rates of morpho-syntactic and phonological feature production were the measures used to make comparisons among contexts and social status characteristics, and these have been calculated in a number of ways (Oetting & McDonald, 2002). Improving understanding of these orderly differences in feature production rates both within and across students lays the foundation for the examination of other skill sets, such as reading and writing. Variations in AAE feature production rates are discussed further in chapter 5 and AAE as an area of Applied Linguistics in chapter 9.

THE DEVELOPMENT OF NONDISCRIMINATORY LANGUAGE AND LITERACY EVALUATION PROCEDURES

The last decade has provided practitioners with a growing number of language evaluation instruments that are appropriate for African American students. These have derived from a number of sources and motivations. First, the search for features and their distributional properties has depended upon being able to distinguish between children with typical or atypical language development. An important by-product of the linguistic and sociolinguistic approaches to the study of child AAE speakers, therefore, has been the development of nondiscriminatory language evaluation procedures. These include traditional approaches to the analysis of spontaneous language samples, for example: the calculation of average production unit lengths (Craig et al., 1998a) and characterizations of complex syntax (Craig & Washington, 1994; Jackson & Roberts, 2001).

Second, African American students are increasingly included in the participant samples of many language studies whose focus is not on dialect or minority student performance. A number of tasks developed for particular language laboratory purposes are proving informative for African American students, and being recommended for culture-fair evaluation purposes. For example, the Nonword Repetition Task (NRT), a well-established language-processing task, has been recommended as a way to remove potential performance effects related to differential experiences with test content and test formats (Campbell, Dollaghan, Needleman, & Janosky, 1997; Oetting & Cleveland, in press; Rodekohr & Haynes, 2001). In other research programs, widely used formal tests like the Peabody Picture Vocabulary Test–Revised (PPVT–R, Dunn & Dunn, 1981) have been found to be discriminatory (Washington & Craig, 1992), consequently have been changed by the test developers (PPVT–III, Dunn & Dunn, 1997), and fare much better in terms of cultural appropriateness for African American students (Washington & Craig, 1999). Lastly, the federal government, specifically the National Institutes of Health, recognized the need for a receptive and expressive test that evaluated the grammar of AAE-speaking students in a comprehensive way. Recently, the Diagnostic Evaluation of Language Variation (DELV, Seymour, Roeper, & de Villiers, 2003) has been published to meet this need.

Overall, tremendous growth has been made in the last decade in the development of language evaluation instruments appropriate for AAE-speaking students. Practitioners can expect that informal evaluation methods will continue to become available as researchers pursue the search for unique features of AAE and for the distributional effects of various rates of feature production. Fortunately, accepted research practice now requires the inclusion of minorities in most studies, suggesting that understanding about discriminatory and nondiscriminatory tasks and procedures will continue to improve.

UNDERSTANDING THE CHALLENGES FACED BY THE AAE-SPEAKING STUDENT IN ACADEMIC CONTEXTS

As is discussed in subsequent chapters, many African American students fail to acquire more than the most basic levels of reading skill. Difficulty learning to read negatively impacts reading to learn academic content from texts. The ultimate result is lower levels of academic achievement for poor readers with potentially lifelong consequences.

A number of factors influence poor reading skills. As discussed in more detail in the final chapters of this book, poverty, family literacy practices, and lower quality classrooms all have been implicated in the difficulties faced by many African American students in attaining higher levels of academic achievement. A major line of research for African American students, therefore, addresses the factors involved in poor academic achievement (e.g., Charity, Scarborough, & Griffin, 2004; Craig & Washington, 2004a; Gutman, Sameroff, & Eccles, 2002; Purcell-Gates, 1996; Stevenson, Chen, & Uttal, 1990) and in developing effective instructional strategies to ameliorate the potential effects of risk factors (e.g., Foorman, Francis, Fletcher, Schatschneider, & Mehta, 1998; Foorman & Torgesen, 2001; Robinson, Larsen, & Haupt, 1996). Furthermore, strong linguistic skills are associated with better reading outcomes for African American students (Charity et al., 2004; Craig & Washington, 2004a; Thompson & Craig, 2005), and offers a largely unexplored venue for developing new, culture-specific approaches to improving literacy acquisition and academic achievement.

THE PLACE OF OUR RESEARCH PROGRAM AT THE UNIVERSITY OF MICHIGAN

Our research program fits squarely within the sociolinguistic approach to the study of AAE-speaking students. As shown in subsequent chapters, our contributions have been to the development of a child AAE feature inventory, the identification of systematic intrinsic and extrinsic sources of variation that influence feature production rates by context, the creation and testing of informal and formal language and literacy evaluation methods, and the examination of the role of language-literacy relationships in the academic achievement of African American students.

Our program of research since 1994 has been conducted in Southeastern Lower Michigan, in an urban-fringe community and a mid-size central city. An intensive and sustained effort to understand African American students residing in these communities has allowed us to build a sequential program of research rather than conduct individual studies. We have benefited from the cohesion of effort and resources and the continuity of questioning that only an ongoing, long-term programmatic approach to research can permit. It is not clear, however, how broadly our findings can be generalized beyond these communities, and this represents an important limitation of the work to date. Unfortunately, this limitation characterizes most of the work to date as the major research programs addressing these issues are housed in different geographic locales. However, looking broadly across the research sites, we see considerable convergence of data. Notably, the child AAE features are the same whether the children reside in the Northeast, South, Southwest, West and northern Midwest. Differences in time of emergence for some features are apparent as well, for example, the remote past feature used by Southerners (Oetting & McDonald, 2001) and northern Midwesterners (Washington & Craig, 1994). In order to better understand how to generalize specific findings to the national context, it will be important for future research to identify regional differences.

We challenge you, the reader, therefore, in subsequent chapters, to consider how applicable the findings we report are to the students with whom you work. To what extent do students in your community produce the features in the inventory? Do students differ in the rates of feature production by context and by age/grade, gender, family socioeconomic status, and community type in the same ways that we have found for our Southeastern Lower Michigan students? Are the evaluation methods we discuss applicable to the African American students in your community, or are alternative locally generated norms necessary? What local factors contribute to the academic achievement of African American students in your own community? And finally, are the implications for future research valid for your own home and work communities, and if not, how can you contribute to this agenda?

3

OUR SCHOOL-BASED PARTICIPANTS AND SAMPLING PROCEDURES

This chapter describes the children who have participated in our ongoing research program and the language sampling methods we used to help us begin to understand their oral language skills. More detail about the methods, and examples of language transcripts and coding systems are provided in Appendix A.

PARTICIPANTS

Approximately 1,000 students have participated in our research program over the past decade and more than half of these (57%) were preschoolers and kindergartners. Most students have been residents primarily of two different northern midwestern communities in Michigan: an urban-fringe community and a mid-size central city. The demographics of the total sample of participants that forms the basis for this book are summarized in Tables 3.1 and 3.2. The urban-fringe community, like other communities in large urban areas, suffers from low student reading achievement. Although the scores on state standards testing are higher for the mid-size central city (69.5% passing) compared to the average for the State of Michigan (60.7%), like other Midwest college towns (Minority Student Achievement Network), this city struggles with a significant Black–White Test Score Gap (77.8%–40.2%, respectively). How can large urban centers like Detroit, Michigan or Los Angeles, California, where potential educational resources are so sparse, resolve the Black–White Achievement Gap, when college towns like Ann Arbor,

TABLE 3.1
Distributional Characteristics of Our Participant Sample (n = 1007)

Grade		Gender		SES		Community	
Pre-K	57%	Male	48%	LSES	46%	Urban-fringe	76%
1–5	43%	Female	52%	MSES	54%	Mid-size central	24%

TABLE 3.2
Selected Demographic Characteristics for Students from Each
of the Two School Districts and for the State of Michigan in 2002

	Urban-fringe	Mid-size central	Michigan
% African American students	85.9	15.6	6.1
% African American students passing MEAP Reading at 4th grade	41.4	40.2	37.9
% White students passing MEAP Reading at 4th grade	37.5[a]	77.8	63.5
% all students passing MEAP Reading at 4th grade	41.5	69.5	60.7
% low income	55.5	16.0	30.7
Median income of communities	$45,460	$51,211	$45,839
$ spent per pupil	$10,811	$10,618	$9,957

Note. From Standard & Poor's School Evaluation Services.
[a]White students in the urban-fringe community are Chaldean-American.

Michigan and Madison, Wisconsin, with tremendous resources cannot do so?

When achievement data are disaggregated by race, more than one third of the African American students in the mid-size central city fail to achieve basic literacy levels at fourth grade, as measured by the state achievement test, the Michigan Educational Assessment Program (MEAP). Both communities, therefore, represent the two types of difficulties facing educators in a variety of school districts across the nation, namely low achievement by students in communities where most students are African American, or a significant Black–White Test Score Gap in resource-rich communities.

The school districts in these two communities share important similarities, which offered us a strong advantage for research design control purposes. It is noteworthy that the urban-fringe community was not a poor school district lacking in resources. Both communities spend slightly more on average per student then the State as a whole. In a context of adequate resources, why aren't the African American students performing better in these two communities? Of special importance for our research program, both districts have very similar and low percentages of African Americans passing the MEAP Reading. For the urban-fringe community, these low achievement levels are consistent with the district data as a whole, where

African American students constitute most of the student body. For the mid-size central city, the low achievement levels of the African American students occur in the context of most students in the district passing the state test, and very high overall achievement for the district as a whole (96th percentile) relative to the rest of the state. Both distributions are indicators of a significant Black–White Test Score Gap.

The two districts also offer our research program potentially informative points of contrast. Both districts enroll quite comparable numbers of African American students, approximately 3,500 in the urban-fringe community and 2,600 in the mid-size central city. In the urban-fringe community, however, African American students are in the majority whereas in the mid-size central city they are in the minority (see Table 3.2).

Gender and SES have been allowed to vary in recruiting participants to our research program. Despite no selection criteria specific to gender, approximately half of the participant sample was male. In addition, despite no selection criteria based on SES, between 45% and 55% of the participant sample each year was from low socioeconomic status (LSES) homes and 48% from middle socioeconomic status (MSES) homes.

SES was determined by students' participation or nonparticipation in the federally funded free or reduced-price lunch program and scores derived from the Hollingshead Four Factor Index of Social Status (Hollingshead, 1975). The Hollingshead Index, which was based on questionnaires that were completed by caregivers, assigned points for occupational status, level of schooling completed, marital status, and gender of the primary caregiver. Points were converted to a single score that corresponded with one of five levels, which was an index of a family's socioeconomic status.

It has often been reported that recruitment of African American students for research is complicated by the low-income status of families. Early research studies of the 1960s and 1970s focused primarily on inner city schools (Fasold, 1972; Harber, 1977; Labov, Cohen, Robins, & Lewis, 1968; Torrey, 1972). Our participant sample has been remarkably balanced relative to SES. We have not had families from low-income homes avoid our research program. This is due in large part to prioritizing a visible presence in the communities in which we collected data. For more than a decade, research staff provided leadership to school districts in the form of teacher meetings, parent workshops, and professional development opportunities for principals and administrators. When asked, staff provided speech-language assessments to children who might not meet our inclusion criteria but were of concern to classroom teachers or other professionals, along with individual consultations and follow-up as needed. Whether in the program or not, at times all children entering preschool or kindergarten were screened by the research staff when needed by the school districts. We continue to maintain an open door policy for any faculty, staff, or parent in the participating school districts. Often we are asked how we are able to include so many children in our research program, and how we are able to conduct our program of research with so little resistance. The answer is: We work hard at it! The district administrators know that they are receiving many hours of high-quality service at no direct cost, in exchange for their participation and cooperation.

As we have suggested elsewhere (Craig, 1996; Craig & Washington, 2004b; Washington & Craig, 2001), it is important to study the language and literacy of African American students from both LSES and MSES homes to avoid attributing potentially confounding effects of poverty to the population as a whole. It is not helpful to associate low achievement with intractable poverty when students from middle-income homes underachieve as well. The educational system must resolve the Black–White Test Score Gap. It would be a disservice to these students and families to minimize this responsibility by attributing the primary sources to factors outside of the control of schools. "No child should be left behind" (No Child Left Behind Act, 2002).

DATA COLLECTION

The majority of our data were collected in school contexts, and mostly on a pullout evaluation basis where a child interacted one-on-one with an adult examiner for up to 1 hour, for potentially two sessions. Like many research programs, the children enjoyed these interactions, and rarely did a child decline to participate.

All data were collected by female examiners who had backgrounds in speech and language, linguistics, developmental psychology, and/or early childhood education. All had some prior experience working with young children. In the early years of the research program, all examiners were African American. As discussed in chapter 5, however, like others (Oetting & McDonald, 2002), we failed to find that race of examiner exerted any systematic influence on the targeted performances of students in preschool through fifth grade. Consequently, both African American and White examiners have administered the data collection protocol in recent years. Indeed, at the later grades when school-based language and literacy behaviors are increasingly our focus of inquiry, White examiners represent the more ecologically valid discourse context. Few (2.2%) speech-language clinicians are African American (American Speech-Language-Hearing Association). Despite the increased percentage of students who are racially and ethnically diverse, there remains little diversity in the teacher pool. Teachers across the nation are more likely to be White females (Toppo, 2003). Comparing today with past generations, Toppo stated:

Minority students account for four in 10 public school kids. One in five speaks a language other than English at home, and 1 in 4 comes from a single parent household. But wait: There's still a White, middle-aged woman at the head of the class. (p. D01)

As NEA President Reg Weaver, who is Black, was quoted in the same *USA Today* article, "The sad reality is that a young boy could go through his entire education without ever having a teacher that looks like me" (Toppo, 2003, p. D01).

Spontaneous Language Sampling Contexts

Collecting representative language samples from students requires attention to their changing interactional skills, and to the increasing external demands placed on them for effective communication across more academic contexts. During the early years of our research program, when we focused primarily on preschoolers and kindergartners, the primary data collection context was a 15 to 20 minute spontaneous oral language sample elicited during free play with toys. Three toy sets were created for language sampling purposes. They were comprised of action figures, dolls, and the Fisher-Price school. Rather than controlling for the specific items with which each child played, we attempted to control for interest level. Accordingly, each child was presented with the three toy sets, and each was allowed to select which one to use during the free play. In almost all cases, the child's interest in the toys and the 15 to 20 minute sample durations were successful in eliciting an adequate corpus of dialogue for analysis purposes. Our goal in these interactions was to engage the child in conversation. Accordingly, the examiner followed the child's lead, assuming roles in play as appropriate, and asked open-ended questions designed to elicit rich descriptive statements and elaborated talk as the activity unfolded. The examiner avoided overusing yes–no questions, which can result in no more than a series of stereotypical "yes" and "no" from the child. We continue to sample free play interactions with preschoolers and kindergartners.

As our research program expanded to include elementary-grade students up through Grade 5, we adopted picture descriptions as another primary data collection context. Picture descriptions are semistructured language elicitation contexts. The set of vocabulary and verb relationships are supported by the objects and actions in the pictures and thus provide support for the child's linguistic formulations. What the child says is not prescribed, however, as it might be in highly structured sampling contexts like elicited imitation. Charity, Scarborough, and Griffin (2004), for example, used elicited imitation techniques and asked students to repeat exactly sentences like *The girl behind him is called Lisa*, immediately after the examiner presented it. Highly structured language contexts like imitation of a prior adult utterance may not correlate well with spontaneous usage for some children (Fujiki & Brinton, 1987) or may fail to elicit grammatical formulations within the child's command, and potentially underrepresent a child's linguistic knowledge (Klee, 1992; Prutting, Gallagher, & Mulac, 1975). Compared to free play, picture description is more monologue-like without requiring story grammar knowledge and the additional cognitive demand that establishing referential relationships, creating plots, and so forth would require. For African American children, picture description yields more examples of dialectal features than spontaneous free play (Washington et al., 1998) and thus is a highly efficient elicitation context for these purposes.

Picture descriptions are advantageous at later grades because they have good ecological validity to tasks within classrooms whereas spontaneous free play with toys has less. Describing pictures and using the information gained from pictures is a routine part of instructional pedagogy as well as a device used by children as they acquire reading comprehension skills. Thompson (2003), for example, observed that highly proficient fourth-grade African American readers structured their picture descriptions in ways quite similar to some classroom interactions. She observed that highly proficient readers imposed a structure on their discourse during picture description, using a variety of semantic and syntactic cohesive devices to link ideas and to elaborate the theme of each picture. This self-imposition of structure resulted in the same rich uses of vocabulary and elaborated sentence forms as was elicited during the teacher's scaffolding of students' responses during a social studies lesson. Scaffolding included use of specific prompts and questions that linked directly to the students' discourse. In sum, picture descriptions are naturalistic classroom discourse contexts, are supportive without being linguistically prescriptive, and efficient as an expressive language sampling context.

Examples follow of a free play sample (see Table 3.3) and a picture description sample (see Table 3.4). We used the Accident, Ice Skating, and Crossing Guard pictures from the Bracken Concept Development Program (Bracken, 1986). As discussed later in the chapter, interactions were transcribed, segmented into communication units (C-units, Loban, 1976), and then scored for AAE and complex syntax. As can be seen in these examples, picture description is more monologue-like.

Transcription, Segmentation, and Scoring of Oral Language Samples

All expressive language was transcribed orthographically. As various questions have been addressed within the research program, this has included transcription of oral language samples during free play and picture

TABLE 3.3
A 50 C-Unit Sample of Free Play With Toys
by a Preschool Girl, Lakita, Aged 4;4.17

Adult	Child
	I can't open it.
it opens with the door.	
see this little door?	
	I can't 'cause.
just like this.	
something special's in there.	
what is it?	
looks like you got some dog food and a little trophy.	
	I'm the winner I'm the winner I the winner.
	look I the winner I'm the winner.
huh? you're the winner?	
what did you win?	
	put the dog food.
how did you get that trophy?	
	I feded the dog lots of food.
with the dog food?	
	yes.
yeah?	
where's the dog though?	
I don't see I see a cat.	
	it's the dog.
	so I'm the little girls.
oh what's your name little girl?	
	I don't know.
oh your name is Lakita?	
	yes.
oh your mommy looks so nice.	
you have such a nice.	
	who mommy?
aren't you the mommy of the little of that little girl?	
	no I'm the little girl right here.
that's not your little girl?	
	I no this this is my mommy.
oh that is your mommy.	
I see.	
	oh that my daddy right here.
I see.	
daddy's just sitting on the couch.	
	baby see.
	now gotta go get some shoes on.
	come on mommy.
	go get you some shoes.
	and go in the car.
	oh got me some shoes on.
	got 'em got 'em.

(Continued)

TABLE 3.3
(*Continued*)

Adult	Child
I think there might be some shoes in here too.	
	mom you got shoes in here.
oh yeah you can't go without shoes on.	
	oh look.
yeah you know what?	
you really should brush that hair 'cause it's lookin' a little messy if you ask me.	
	mom.
how do you think my hair looks?	
you think it's ok?	
	um nappy.
it looks well then what are we going to do about that?	
	I'm 'a comb it down.
yeah get that comb it down so it's not nappy anymore right?	
	mmhm.
oh thank you.	
now it looks so pretty.	
	okay now we comb my hair.
what what would you like to eat?	
	boom boom huh?
what should we eat for dinner?	
I think I'm kind of hungry for dinner.	
	um frenchfries and hamburgers.
frenchfries and what?	
	hamburger and frenchfries.
you know.	
while you comb the hair I think I'm gonna make some food in the kitchen.	
	okay go ahead.
burger and frenchfries?	
	yes.
mmm that sounds good.	
	ooh this shoes I like.
	look mama.
ooh those are very pretty.	
except how are you gonna walk?	
	I don't know baby.
	look mommy.
ooh I really like those.	
those look good for walkin'.	
	I know.
yeah I was thinking that maybe after we eat dinner we could go take a walk since you put your shoes on.	
	so them wanna walk too.

(*Continued*)

TABLE 3.3
(Continued)

Adult	Child
and I think the cat might like to go for a walk too.	
think so?	
	the cat?
yeah.	
oh we better stay here for a little bit mommy.	
	over there mommy.
	oh well oh well I just better take a walk myself ok?
you well I'll go with you.	
	okay.
should we go before dinner?	
	yes.
and we'll leave the cat here.	
	yes I need my shoes too.
	need oh you got your shoes?
	my daddy don't got no shoes either.
uhoh that's a problem.	
was he gonna go on the walk too?	
	yes he go on a walk too.

TABLE 3.4

A Sample Picture Description of the Three Pictures by Malik at Preschool

Adult	Child
ok tell me about this picture.	
	it's emergency.
mmhm.	
	and the bike.
mmhm.	
	broke.
	jacket.
	car.
	man.
	lady.
ok.	
what's going on in the picture?	
	somebody got dead off the bike.
	and they hit something.
	this hit the car.
what else?	
	and this put the the jackets.
ok.	
	he had fell.
	and the car runned over him.
ok is that all?	
	and him was go play basketball.

(Continued)

TABLE 3.4
(Continued)

Adult	Child
ok lets try the next one.	
tell me about this picture, Malik.	
	and they knocked the papers over.
	the car did.
	the car did it.
anything else?	
	they stopped the kids from runnin'.
	and they came out the school.
	and from the street.
	the kids runnin' from the street.
ok.	
	and that's how they go &pl they were fitna go back there and play with everything.
ok.	
	he was tryin' to get in the car.
good job Malik.	
tell me about this picture.	
	the peoples skatin' in the &s in the ice.
	and they fell.
	and two and three too.
	and then one and two fell.
	and the other one started skatin'.
	other one started skatin'.
	it was fun.
	and the other one started slide.
	and the &sn and they built a snowman
mmhm.	
	wit snow.
	I can't build snowmans.
	I can't.
	my momma can.
	but I can't.
you can't?	
what else do you see in the picture?	
	I see lots o' kids skatin'.
	'cause they like skatin' in the ice.
good job.	

Note. Pictures taken from the Bracken Concept Development Program (Bracken, 1986).

description, reading aloud, and of written story generation. Expressive language was segmented primarily into C-units, although utterances were also the unit of analysis for our earliest studies with preschoolers (Craig & Washington, 1994, 1995; Washington & Craig, 1994).

Loban's (1976) segmentation criteria for C-units defined a communication unit as an independent clause, plus its modifiers. These modifying clauses could take the form of coordinate, subordinate, or relative clauses. Examples follow.

C-unit with coordinate clause.
I'll play anything in here <u>but not no girl stuff</u>

C-unit with subordinate clause.
I'm gonna change her clothes <u>'cause she been baseballing</u>

C-unit with relative clause.
and somebody helping somebody <u>that's bouta get in a in a icepuddle</u>

More details of the transcription and segmentation processes are provided in Appendix A.

Only wholly intelligible C-units were scored. Whereas most of the participants in our research program have been students with typical language development, most students have been highly intelligible. All transcripts of oral language production were scored for the student's production of AAE features and for complex syntax constructions. The AAE features are presented in chapter 4.

Transcription and scoring reliabilities were established for every transcript. A portion of an audiotape was retranscribed and rescored by independent individuals who were not involved in creation of the original transcripts or scores. Statistical treatments facilitated interpretations of the data obtained. Data were analyzed using statistical analysis software, SPSS.

SUMMARY

The methods and procedures described in this chapter were carefully developed to permit culture-fair assessment and interpretation of our data. The urban-fringe and mid-size central communities were selected for inclusion because they represent a critical cross-section of African American families, ranging from urban to suburban, low to middle income, single parent to multigenerational, and from high school dropouts to college graduates. Using the methods described herein we have been successful in recruiting a representative sample of African American students whose oral language performance has provided the basis for development of culturally sensitive elicitation procedures, as well as a culture-fair assessment protocol that is presented in the chapters that follow.

4

FEATURES OF CHILD AAE

This chapter discusses the features of child AAE. The chapter begins by laying the groundwork for the processes involved in discovering the features used by typically developing African American children, especially the challenges involved in this type of research. The features are then identified and described briefly. More detail and examples are provided in Appendix B.

This language sample presented in Table 4.1 was collected from Malik at 9 years old. Malik's description of the Ice Skating picture (Bracken, 1986) exemplifies the extensive production of AAE that we see by fourth graders in his urban school district. Even in this brief sample, 6 of his 7 communication units (C-units) included an AAE feature. Malik's language sample underscores the importance of understanding the young student's production of AAE, because dialect features can be so much a part of his or her typical sentence formulation.

BACKGROUND ISSUES

The Uniqueness of Child AAE

Often, when we present information about the AAE features produced by young students, a member of the listening audience may comment: "I hear Southerners say that." It is the case that AAE is not mutually exclusive from Southern dialect. Southern White dialects and AAE share a complex history so that a number of features are shared by both dialects. For children, Oetting and McDonald (2001) recently identified morpho-syntactic features of rural and Southern dialects spoken by Southern White English- and

TABLE 4.1
A Sample of Malik's Language Production
at Age 9 With Corresponding AAE Codes

Adult	Child
tell me about this picture.	
	ok &uh these people they are skatin'.
	PRO
	G
	and it say danger thin ice.
	SVA
	and they gonna fall.
	COP
what else?	
	that all I can see.
	COP
something else is goin' on.	
	and these people by some fire.
	COP
	some people is by some fire.
	SVA
	that's all I can see.
ok.	

Note. Fragments are indicated by &. AAE morpho-syntactic features include: PRO = Appositive pronoun; SVA = Subject–verb agreement; COP = Zero copula or auxiliary of the verb *to be*. Phonology features include: G = *g*-dropping. Ice Skating picture taken from the Bracken Concept Development Program (Bracken, 1986).

Southern African American English-speaking (SWE and SAAE, respectively) students, who were residents of Southeastern Louisiana. Overlap between the dialects was found to be considerable. The differences manifested themselves primarily as frequency of use differences with SAAE-speaking students producing four verb-based features more frequently than their SWE-speaking peers, including: *zero regular 3rd person, zero be, subject–verb agreement with be,* and *zero regular past tense -ed.* Overlap between AAE and Southern dialects is not surprising given the shared regional history of these two dialects of English. Migrations north by African Americans likely transferred many of the linguistic characteristics of SAAE to northern communities. Northern speakers of child AAE produce different feature patterns than Southern speakers of child AAE. Washington and Craig (1992) found that on the Arizona Articulation Proficiency Scale (Fudala & Reynolds, 1986), the Northern students who were speakers of AAE performed comparably to the standardization sample comprising the test, whereas Southern speakers of child AAE, students from Mississippi (Cole & Taylor, 1990), required a scoring adjustment for features that were clearly characteristic of Southern English dialects.

The extent to which overlap exists between SAAE, and the AAE spoken by students, has not yet been determined but warrants investigation. For these reasons, we document whether parents are first or later generation Northerners. The extent to which students who are at least second-generation Northerners produce features similarly or differently from SAAE speakers would inform theoretical conceptualizations of child AAE.

Current Terminology

The dialect spoken by African Americans is identified by a number of different names. By and large, the names reflect the underlying theoretical assumptions made by the person using the term about the linguistic status of the dialect. *Black English* (BE) is rarely used today, but was a frequent term prior to the widespread adoption of the term African Americans rather than Blacks to identify members of the racial group. As Terrell and Terrell (1993) observed, changes in terminology have corresponded to changes in racial name identification. *African American Vernacular English* (AAVE) is a term used by linguists (Labov, Baker, Bullock, Ross, & Brown, 1998; Rickford, 1997; Winford, 1997; Wolfram, 1994), and reflects assumptions that the dialect is a vernacular or informal register characterizing conversational interactions, but not more formal types of discourse. Unlike other terms, *Ebonics* (Abati, 1997; Baron, 2000; Perry & Delpit, 1998; Rickford, 1999) became a highly politicized term after the "Ebonics Debate" of 1994. Use of the term Ebonics often reflects the speaker's assumptions that the dialect is diverging from SAE. By implication, its divergence is resulting in a linguistic system that differs so much from SAE that it should be considered a separate language with its own unique name.

In our research program, we have adopted the term *African American English* (AAE), which we believe best represents the nature of the dialect spoken by children. For students, we avoid AAVE because for young children it may imply a choice that isn't theirs. They do not yet possess a repertoire of linguistic alternatives. *Vernacular* emphasizes an informal discourse status, characteristic of oral conversation. African American students, however, produce AAE not just in spoken discourse but also during reading and writing (Thompson et al., 2004). Ebonics emphasizes the divergence from SAE. In contrast, we believe that AAE is a creolized process that represents the merger of languages. AAE is an advantageous term because it captures the magnitude of the variations from SAE, and unlike Ebonics, AAE highlights continuing important relationships to English as the parent language.

It is unfortunate that the term *dialect* is used by proponents of all of these points of view. English dialects take two forms: the merger of a language like Spanish with English, and changes in English related to geographic regions. The r-lessness of the Northeastern United States, in which "*park the car*" is pronounced as "*pa_k the ca_*" is an example of a regional dialect. Unlike regional dialects, however, merged languages such as AAE are not just a small set of variations representing primarily phonological differences. AAE is a comprehensive set of variations from SAE, and includes prosodic, phonological, morpho-syntactic, lexical, and discourse types, many of which are associated with unique and dialect-specific meanings (Green, 2002; Martin & Wolfram, 1998). Referring to AAE as a dialect minimizes the substantive changes involved in the merger of two languages. The term dialect then may lead the layperson to believe that these variations exert few important influences, much like the limited impact of regional variations for pronunciation in other U.S. dialects. As will be discussed in later chapters, AAE, however, does impact language and literacy acquisition in broad and significant ways. The reader is encouraged to read more about creolization and the merger of African languages with English. See for example: Bailey, Maynor, and Cukor-Avila, 1991; Rickford, 1998; Winford, 1997. It is important to remember that the term dialect, which is widely used, is a general term adopted by proponents of a diverse set of theoretical perspectives. Like others, we use the term dialect as a general referent to AAE throughout the book.

Challenges to Identifying AAE Features for Children

Two major challenges must be faced in identifying features produced by young African American students: distinguishing those variations that are developmental rather than dialectal, and distinguishing those variations that alternatively may be symptomatic of a language disorder. At a surface level, both developmental and clinical sources of variation often are indistinguishable from AAE features.

AAE Features and Developmental Patterns

Most dialectal research prior to the 1990s was focused on older adolescents and adults at a time when the research priority was to disprove a prevailing and misguided assumption that AAE was a deficient form of SAE. This was a foundational and foremost issue and represented considerable investigative effort (Dillard, 1972; Fasold & Wolfram, 1970; Stewart, 1970; Wolfram, 1971; Wolfram & Fasold, 1974). The mature language systems of older linguistically competent adolescents and adults offered the most appropriate language corpus for these studies, and yielded a number of taxonomies consistent with adult usage.

Relying on adult models for child AAE features has merit when no other starting point is available. The study of child language acquisition has depended upon this approach since its inception. For example, during the 1960s and 1970s when developmental psycholinguistics was emerging as a new discipline, important foundational descriptions of child language (Brown, 1973; Brown, Cazden, & Bellugi, 1968; Klima & Bellugi, 1966; Lee, 1974; McNeill, 1970; Miller & Ervin-Tripp, 1964, etc.) derived their analyses from Chomsky's (1957) theory of mature language functioning.

Similarly, child language researchers interested in African American students applied the taxonomies derived from the study of mature AAE systems to the analysis of the discourse of children. Morpho-syntactic AAE features were the focus of this fairly large body of early work. The work of Baratz (1970) offers one of the earliest examples of an application of the mature AAE feature system to the study of young children. Unfortunately, many of the resulting studies from this era were preliminary in nature or not widely disseminated (Blake, 1984; Bridgeforth, 1984; Cole, 1980; Kovac, 1980; Reveron, 1978; Steffensen, 1974; Stokes, 1976) and thus had little impact on the fields of speech–language pathology and early education.

As new and important child taxonomies have been published for mainstream speakers, they also have been applied to the study of African American children. Stockman and Vaughn-Cooke (1982, 1984; Stockman, 1984) applied Bloom and Lahey's (1978) content-form-use taxonomy to the discourse of AAE-speaking children. More recently, Nelson (1993; Nelson & Hyter, 1990) applied Lee's (1974) *Developmental Sentence Scoring* to the study of African American children.

It is not debatable that child AAE is developmental. AAE does not emerge in children's discourse fully developed in the adult form of the dialect, any more than one would expect this for an SAE-speaking child. The features change as the student matures. Most of what we do know about the changes in AAE over time derive primarily from distributional analyses and will be discussed later in the next chapter.

Although in our research program we have found that young children produce most of the features used by the adults in their linguistic community, there are important differences (Washington & Craig, 2002). For example, adult AAE includes a feature in which there is noninversion of subject and auxiliary for yes–no questions (e.g., Adult: *It's gonna be a surprise?*). Noninversion in wh-question forms is infrequent for adults. In contrast for children, most noninversions occur as part of a wh-question form (e.g., Child: *what I'm gonna do with mine?*). (See Washington and Craig [2002] for additional discussion of the noninverted question feature.) The linguistic systems of young students are still developing in fundamental ways, so it is not surprising that child AAE, characterized by morpho-syntactic and phonological features, is not identical to that of the mature language users of the children's homes and same communities. It has been important to study child AAE in its own right. When only adult models drive the description of child AAE, information remains critically incomplete. A comprehensive understanding of child AAE has required a child-centered approach.

A Child-Centered Linguistic Strategy
for the Study of Child AAE

The work of the great linguist Kenneth Pike (1967) provides an informative heuristic for the study of new dimensions of child language, and we have adopted his strategy for our study of child AAE. Pike differentiated between two types of analytical units: etic and emic units. Etic units were defined as those available in advance, prior to the beginning of analysis, and offered a starting point, whereas emic units were those discovered during the process of analysis. Consideration of both levels of inquiry has been invaluable in our studies of child AAE.

Essentially, the etic–emic approach to child AAE can be conceptualized as first the etic phase, in which variations from SAE are identified based on pre-existing taxonomies for adult AAE features. There are a wealth of these systems and a large and rich literature available that characterizes the mature African American speaker to guide this etic process for children (e.g., Dillard, 1972; Fasold & Wolfram, 1970; Labov, 1970, 1972). Next, the emic phase adopts a child-centered approach by cataloguing all variations from SAE that are not identifiable as AAE features based on adult scoring criteria. These apparently anomalous forms are then examined in terms of their distributional properties across large numbers of students. Consequently, we considered anomalous forms to be additional instances of AAE feature production, but child versions of the forms if they met the following three criteria: (a) the linguistic behavior bears some correspondence to adult forms, (b) the behavior is widely dispersed across students, and (c) the child form lends itself to a developmental explanation. As a result, our taxonomy for child AAE consists of forms that are identical to those reported for adults (from the etic phase of analysis), and additional child forms, which bear a relationship to the later mature forms (from the emic phase of analysis).

Our analysis of children's productions of the *double modal* feature provides an example of application of the etic–emic process, and the identification of a child form of the feature. The extant literature for adults identifies a *double modal* feature in which two modal auxiliary forms are produced in a single clause, for example, *I might could*. (This is a characteristic of Southern dialects as well.) We have not found this feature in the discourse of preschoolers and kindergartners, no doubt because developmentally, for most children acquiring English, modals are still being acquired at the time of school entry. However, we do see young African American students produce multiples of copulas and auxiliaries, verb constituents that they have mastered at school entry. Sentences like: *I'm is the last one ridin' on*, suggest that this is a child form of the adult feature. Double copulas/auxiliaries are not part of the descriptions of the adult feature system, but are widely dispersed across children, and serve essentially the same syntactic role that *double modals* will for older students and adults. In our research program, only one child prior to fourth grade produced the double modal feature saying during free play: *she might can wear these*, while playing with dolls. Our child data have provided no examples of *might could* as is more typically reported for adults. It would be interesting in future research to probe for the development of this feature and other complex modals and auxiliary verbs such as *have been* in the language systems of AAE-speaking children.

Most existing research has focused on syntactic and morphological features for both adults and children. Therefore, this was our starting point as well (Washington & Craig, 1994). Morpho-syntactic features are discussed in more depth later in this chapter. Only recently have we addressed phonological features, and phonological analyses of child AAE present a special significant challenge. The *cluster reduction* feature exemplifies the difficulties inherent in distinguishing dialectal from developmental linguistic behaviors. *Cluster reduction* is an often-cited feature for mature speakers of AAE (Stockman, 1996; Wolfram, 1994), and *cluster reductions* are also readily apparent in the discourse of African American students (Craig, Thompson, et al., 2003).

Elementary-grade students participating in our research program frequently produce cluster reductions while reading aloud. For example, they may change "mind" to what sounds like "mine" by reducing the /nd/ to /n/. It is a straightforward deduction that this change reflects operation of the *cluster reduction* feature when other aspects of the discourse evidence intentional cluster reduction. For example, when a student contracts "it is" to the cluster "it's" this is a morpho-syntactic rather than phonologically driven change. Students who produce both contracted and uncontracted forms demonstrate that they have the motor skill necessary either to produce the full forms, or to make an optional reduction. In contrast, it is difficult to ascribe feature status to many variations that are phonological in nature when students are young and both the oral–motor and morpho-syntactic systems are still immature, as in preschool and kindergarten. We have begun the study of phonological features but have focused on older, motorically more mature elementary-grade students to eliminate any potential confounds in these first analyses. Future research should address the AAE features produced by very young children. Now that an elementary-grade taxonomy is available, the older AAE-speaking student can provide the etic basis for a scaled down and comprehensive first look at preschoolers and kindergartners. Clearly a focused and sustained inquiry into the development of all aspects of child AAE is warranted. Information is needed on the linguistic sequencing of AAE features so that the child's variations from SAE are not misunderstood.

Intensive inquiry into the development of AAE may provide additional insights into the cognitive–linguistic processes required for feature acquisitions and their timing. One cognitive–linguistic process important for understanding child AAE will be the development of optionality as part of the

AAE feature system. For example, we see occasional attachment errors, such as *which one do_ it goes on?*" and the basis for these attachment errors is unclear. A likely explanation rests in developmental processes, related to the optionality of features like *subject–verb agreement variations*. Acquiring morphological forms that are characterized by optionality may be linguistically more difficult and thus later developing.

Perhaps attachment errors represent a developmental stage in the acquisition of AAE, in which the child attaches the optional morphological form to a main verb rather than to the auxiliary as in the preceding example. The main verb will always be present in this type of sentence construction, whereas the auxiliary in many AAE constructions can be expressed or not. Attaching the subject–verb agreement marker *-es* to the main verb, which in a sense is the verb constituent on which the student can depend, would ground some of the optional variation in the formulation.

Improving our understanding of the ways in which African American students manage the increased cognitive demands of a linguistic system rich in optionality, and the timing of these acquisition substages, would be of interest to researchers characterizing dialect, and to practitioners involved in language-based academic planning for young children. The foregoing discussion is highly speculative but is presented to underscore the lack of information we continue to have about child AAE, and to demonstrate that the findings may be very interesting ones. Too little is known about the developmental course of AAE, and about ways to support the acquisition of new morphological forms for children acquiring the dialect. Intensive descriptive longitudinal research would be important to this process and remains forthcoming.

AAE Features and Characteristics of Language Impairments

Many of the behaviors associated with specific language impairment (SLI) reflect morpho-syntactic difficulties (Gopnick & Crago, 1991; Leonard, 1998; Rice & Oetting, 1993; Rice, Wexler, & Cleave, 1995). At a surface level, these difficulties overlap with the formulations represented by some AAE features. The most common features of AAE for both middle-SES and low-SES students are *zero copula*, in which copula and auxiliary forms of the verb *to be* are variably included and excluded (e.g., *the bridge _ out* and *I _ not finished eatin' yet*), and *variations in subject–verb agreement*, in which number can vary between the subject and the verb (e.g., *I gets too hot*). The DELV was developed to permit more reliable identification of children who are AAE speakers and who use zero-marked forms that have been problematic for characterization of childhood SLI. Although this instrument represents a breakthrough in our ability to assess AAE-speaking children, our knowledge of the linguistic rule structure represented by these zero-marked forms remains incomplete and important to understand.

Tense marking consistently distinguishes typically developing students from those with SLI who are SAE speakers (Rice & Wexler, 1996), and Rice and Wexler (1996) have proposed that omissions of 3rd person singular *-s*, regular past tense *-ed*, the verb *be*, and the primary auxiliary *do* are all strong candidates for clinical markers of language disorder. A clinical marker is a linguistic form that reliably distinguishes between children with SLI and their typically developing peers. In 1998, Rice presented the utterances below (in column one) as examples of clinically significant tense errors. Alternatively (in the adjacent column), we have identified AAE features that might be associated with these variations from SAE if the speaker were African American.

Rice's examples	*Potential AAE features*
1. Patsy walk	*zero past tense* or *subject–verb agreement*
2. Yesterday Patsy walk home after work	*zero past tense*
3. Patsy walking	*zero copula*
4. Patsy happy	*zero copula*
5. Patsy work today?	*zero copula* and *zero -ing*; or *zero auxiliary*
6. Patsy likes to walks	
7. Patsy made him walks	
8. The dogs walks	

Whereas the DELV provides a means to identify AAE-speaking children who are having language difficulty, the utterances illustrate, at the level of morpho-syntax, distinctions between AAE and current proposals for clinical markers are not possible.

Why is this the case? A simple explanation is that there are only so many things one can do to the basic language forms of English, so it is not surprising that there is overlap. One would not expect a child with SLI, for example, to be using forms characteristic of a language other than English. Furthermore, consistent with some theories of language disorder, clinical markers may be early developmental forms that do not mature and evolve. More recently, Rice (2003) and others (Crago & Paradis, 2003) have described these grammatical deficits in children with SLI as evidence of a period of *extended optional infinitive* (EOI). The EOI stage is based on Poeppel and Wexler's (1993) hypothesis that there is a maturational stage in normal development during which finite and nonfinite verb forms are used optionally because tense has not been acquired. In the case of children with SLI,

Rice (2003) suggests that grammatical tense markers are evident at a later age, show a slower rate of acquisition, but follow a typical trajectory toward the adult grammar that is not different from normal controls. As de Villiers (2003) appropriately notes, this focus on tense and agreement in grammatical markers of SLI is problematic because of the significant overlap with the communication skills of children who use AAE.

Considerable additional information is needed about the acquisition processes involved in AAE but the fact that it is developmental and that optionality is a hallmark of the dialectal system distinguishes it from the clinical characteristics of SLI. AAE variations from SAE, therefore, are quite different, despite any apparent sentence surface level similarities in forms.

It may be that tense errors offer a clinical marker only for SAE and cannot be generalized beyond mainstream speakers of English. The concept of a clinical marker for SLI is most powerful if it has more universal application than for just SAE speakers. More and more information is becoming available about tense errors as clinical markers for language impairment (Leonard, 1995, 1998; Loeb & Leonard, 1991; Rice & Oetting, 1993; Rice & Wexler, 1996; Rice et al., 1995). Therefore, we must avoid repeating the mistakes of the past and be sure that AAE features, particularly the omission of tense markers, are not viewed as deviant or inferior forms of SAE. If tense as a clinical marker only applies to SAE, then this needs to be made explicit. The search for clinical markers for AAE-speaking students is a critical research imperative at this time.

WHAT ARE THE FEATURES OF AAE FOR PRESCHOOLERS THROUGH FIFTH GRADERS?

Our current understanding of the characteristics of child AAE is rooted in our understanding of the morpho-syntactic features. This feature system has been the focus of considerable intensive inquiry over the last decade or so, and considerable new information has been gained (Craig & Washington, 2002; Washington & Craig, 1994, 1998, 2002). Recently, a comprehensive taxonomy for child phonological features has been published as well (Craig, Thompson, et al., 2003). The prosodic and pragmatic aspects of child AAE, across all grades, remain largely unknown at this time. The remainder of this chapter describes the morpho-syntactic and phonological features of child AAE.

Morpho-Syntactic Features of Child AAE

The morpho-syntactic feature system includes the variations from SAE that involve free and bound morphemes, and word order. Additional comments and examples are available in Appendix B. The 24 morpho-syntactic features used by preschoolers through fifth graders within our research program are the following.

Ain't. *Ain't* used as a negative auxiliary in *are+not*, *is+not*, *have+not*, and *do+not* constructions.

Appositive pronoun. A pronoun is used in addition to a noun, or a second pronoun, to signify the same referent.

Completive *done*. *Done* and *did* used to emphasize a recently completed action.

Double marking. Multiple agreement markers are used for irregular plural nouns, pronouns (especially possessive pronoun mines), and hyper-correction of irregular verbs. For children, these double mark number or verb tense.

Double copula/auxiliary/modal. Two modal auxiliary forms, used in a single clause, is a feature of adult AAE. For children, two copula or auxiliary forms of the verb *to be* may be produced.

Existential *it*. *It* is produced in place of *there* to indicate the existence of a referent without adding meaning. Picture description is a high frequency context for eliciting this form from children.

Fitna/sposeta/bouta. The words *fixing to*, *supposed to*, and *about to* are produced as abbreviated forms coding imminent action.

Preterite *had*. *Had* is added before simple past verbs.

Indefinite article. *A* is used regardless of whether the onset of the subsequent noun is a vowel.

Invariant *be*. Infinitival *be* is used to express habitual or extended actions and states.

Multiple negation. Two or more negatives are used to express negation. The mixing of positive and negative terms is avoided so that all potential forms for expressing negation are consistently marked.

Regularized reflexive pronoun. *Hisself, theyself, theirselves* replace regular forms of the reflexive pronouns *himself, themselves.*

Remote past *been*. *Been* coding action in the remote past is an AAE feature, but was rarely ever produced by preschoolers or kindergartners in our program of research over the last 10 years.

Subject–verb agreement variations. Subjects and verbs are produced with differences in marking of number. These include omission of the 3rd person singular number marker *-s* on main verbs, and differences in the relationships between subjects and auxiliaries.

Undifferentiated pronoun case. Pronoun cases are used interchangeably. Objective and nominative cases substitute for each other.

Zero article. Articles are variably included and excluded.

Zero copula. *Is, are, am* and other forms of the verb *to be* are variably included or excluded in either copula or auxiliary form.

Zero -*ing*. Present progressive -*ing* is variably included or excluded.

Zero modal auxiliary. *Will, can, do,* and *have* are variably included or excluded as modal auxiliaries.

Zero past tense. The -*ed* marker for simple past is variably included and excluded on regular past verbs. Many may also be considered phonological combination features because cluster reduction is involved (see the next section). Present forms of irregulars are used as well.

Zero plural. The plural -*s* marker on nouns is variably included and excluded, and includes /s/, /z/, and /ɪz/ phonological forms.

Zero possessive. Possession is coded by word order so the possessive -*s* marker is omitted, and includes /s/ and /z/ phonological forms. We also code **zero possessive** when the case of the possessive pronoun is changed, although this might be considered another example of **undifferentiated pronoun case**.

Zero preposition. Prepositions are variably omitted.

Zero *to*. Infinitival *to* is variably included and excluded.

Contrastive Phonological Features of Child AAE

Nine phonological features were used by our first through fifth graders. Using the etic–emic approach, we identified a set of potential features from the extant literature for African American adults. Accordingly, we searched for nine features and found that the students produced all nine features during oral reading and/or discourse. See Appendix B for examples.

The phonological features used by first through fifth graders within our research program are the following.

Consonant cluster movement. The reversal of phonemes within a cluster. This may involve consonant reduplication, or may be a change in order without reduplication.

Devoicing final consonants. Voiceless consonants substitute for voiced following the vowel.

Postvocalic consonant reduction. Consonant singles are omitted following vowels.

"g" dropping. Substitutions of /n/ for /ŋ/.

Substitutions for /θ/ and /ð/. /t/ and /d/ substitute for /θ/ and /ð/ in prevocalic positions and /f, t/ and /v/ substitute for /θ/ and /ð/ in intervocalic and postvocalic positions.

Consonant cluster reduction. Deletion of phonemes that are part of a consonant cluster.

Syllable deletion. Omission of an unstressed syllable in a multisyllabic word.

Syllable addition. Addition of a syllable to a word, usually as a hypercorrection.

Monophthongization of diphthongs. Neutralization of diphthongs.

Combinations of Morpho-Syntactic and Phonological Features

Five of the morpho-syntactic features could combine with two of the phonological features and these were designated as combinations. Labov, Baker, Bullock, Ross, and Brown (1998) argue that *past tense consonant cluster reduction* is a phonological rather than morpho-syntactic rule. However, this proposal has not yet been confirmed and awaits additional research for children. Accordingly, we simply designated these as combinations, and these seven are listed below.

Consonant cluster reduction + zero past tense.

Consonant cluster reduction + zero plural.

Consonant cluster reduction + subject–verb agreement.

Postvocalic consonant reduction + zero past.

Postvocalic consonant reduction + zero plural.

Postvocalic consonant reduction + zero possessive.

Postvocalic consonant reduction + subject–verb agreement.

Some General Observations on the Foregoing Features

Some of the above features seem to be widely dispersed across students. Students use some quite often while others rarely occur, for example, undifferentiated pronoun case, nominative for objective "*me don't know.*" When a more complete understanding of child AAE is available, we may find that some of these forms are low prestige, some are purely developmental, and some may be regional, and that these differences affect their frequencies of use.

In linguistic terms, AAE is considered a low-prestige dialect overall. Furthermore, there remain some who consider AAE to be a poor subtraction of SAE rather than a distinct linguistic system. These views are based in social value statements that are negative toward AAE. Within the linguistic community, many African Americans rank features in terms of social acceptability. Within the dialect itself, there are some specific features that are stigmatizing and considered to be low prestige. Many highly educated African Americans who speak AAE still will not use all features. These include: *ain't*, multiple negatives especially if *ain't* is part of the formulation, *fitna*, /aks/ for "*ask*," *andem* for "*and them*." The low-prestige features of the dialect are primarily lexical/phonological variations from SAE, rather than morpho-syntactic in nature. Additionally, some features are context dependent and can be difficult to detect. For example, postvocalic consonant reduction + zero auxiliary, cannot be distinguished without knowing the target word. Therefore this combination can only be observed in some contexts, for example, during oral reading. An example occurred for a fifth-grade student during oral reading, "*I _ lost my blue book*" when the text stated "*I've lost my blue book*."

Overall, variability in feature production characterizes child AAE. Whether or not a specific feature occurs likely reflects a complex set of influences, which range widely from sociocultural forces to sampling error. Important influences on combined feature production rates are better understood, and are discussed in the next chapter.

SUMMARY

The features described in this chapter were derived from our oral language sampling of preschool through fifth grade, typically developing, AAE-speaking students. The chapter discusses major challenges to determining which variations from SAE reflect the operation of AAE features when so little developmental and clinical information is available for comparisons. Morpho-syntactic, phonological, and combinations of morpho-syntactic and phonological features are identified for child AAE.

5

DISTRIBUTIONAL PROPERTIES OF AAE IN THE EARLY GRADES

It is widely assumed that many African Americans are speakers of AAE (Battle, 1993; Manning & Baruth, 2000). Like other background information on AAE, in particular the specific features discussed in the prior chapter, this assumption emerged from the study of adolescent and adult speakers. Our research program has examined children's production of AAE relative to a number of potentially important influences and this chapter discusses our findings for variables that impact the extent to which students use AAE.

STUDENTS WERE SPEAKERS OF AAE

Malik was a speaker of AAE. In our research program at the University of Michigan, of 1,007 preschool through fifth-grade participants, every student was an AAE speaker. This finding was surprising as the extant literature suggested that many but not all African American participants would be dialect speakers. In related work, for example, Connor (2002) examined the student, teacher, family, and classroom characteristics of 10 preschool classrooms in the same two school districts represented by our larger research program. When prompted to tell a story using a wordless picture book, Connor found that of 62 racially Black preschoolers, 48 spoke AAE, 2 were speakers of English as a Second Language (ESL) born to Nigerian parents, and 12 spoke SAE. In other words, most (77%) of these students at the time of school entry spoke AAE in this context. The children who spoke AAE were more likely to live in the urban-fringe community rather than the mid-size central city.

It is not clear why all of our participants were speakers of AAE, but a few possibilities follow.

1. Our recruitment materials may have encouraged AAE speakers to participate rather than African Americans who were SAE speakers. The following text is an excerpt from the introductory portion of our recruitment letter sent home to families:

> *The Michigan Project on African American Language will be in your school doing a study about language development in African American children. Language skills are important for academic subjects such as reading, and it is important for us to understand which skills are most important so that we can help those children who need it. The information learned from this study will help area school districts plan better for all children.*

Thus, recruitment materials discussed the language used by African American students. Although the materials did not mention dialect, parents may have interpreted the project name within a cultural–linguistic framework, to mean AAE. We did recruit some biracial students (73 in the last 4 years). By virtue of their self-selection for enrollment in our research program, the families of biracial students identified with the African American community. Part of their identification with the African American community indeed may be manifested as speakers of AAE.

2. Most of our examiners were African Americans who spoke AAE to the students. Terrell and Terrell (1993) cautioned that due to cultural mistrust, African American students may be reluctant to talk to White examiners. This is not an explanation for our findings however, because, like others (Isaacs, 1996; Seymour, Ashton, & Wheeler, 1986; Smith, Bradham, Chandler, & Wells, 2000), we did not find that race of examiner influenced outcomes in systematic ways. See Appendix C.

3. Many African Americans are bidialectal, that is, competent speakers of both AAE and SAE. Bidialectalism is an emerging competency for students, most likely the result of schooling (Adler, 1992; Craig & Washington, 2004a; Isaacs, 1996). Perhaps most African American children speak AAE because it is their heritage language and the language of their community. So, early in their schooling experiences they have not yet acquired bidialectal skills. From a child-centered perspective, our task as researchers, therefore, is to explain why and how AAE-speaking children develop SAE. It is obvious why they are speakers of AAE. Some students who become competent in both AAE and SAE may choose to adopt only AAE as their linguistic system, others may treat AAE as an informal register and reserve it only for oral communications among friends and family, and others may adopt SAE only. These practices, however, are only possible at later linguistic stages and grades

when a child's morpho-syntactic and phonological systems are sufficiently well developed that register choices are possible. Many African American students who are acquiring SAE will find this skill of little use at home. Thus, practitioners must consider that learning to speak SAE may be only a circumscribed achievement of limited value to many African American students.

4. Although all of our research participants spoke AAE, they did not do so in all contexts. We have begun to explore the systematic ways in which context influences AAE production in students (Thompson et al., 2004; Washington et al., 1998), but the pragmatics of child AAE are not yet understood very well. If there are large contextual effects associated with AAE production, then the context in which the language sample is elicited will be critical to the data obtained. Differences in elicitation contexts, therefore, may account at least in part for the discrepant findings between Connor's (2002) observations that approximately 20% of African American preschoolers spoke SAE, and our research program which has determined AAE-speaker status from free play or picture description language samples. Contexts that are more literacy-based like Connor's elicit more SAE (Thompson et al., 2004) even in preschool (Washington et al., 1998).

5. Most of the students in our research program, approximately 75%, resided in urban-fringe communities of the Metropolitan Detroit areas. Data were also collected in a mid-size central city. Although segregation has declined over the last 20 years, African Americans experience higher residential segregation than any other group (Iceland, Weinberg, & Steinmetz, 2002). Therefore, community can be a proxy for racial demographics. Not surprisingly, then, the proportion of African Americans residing in our urban-fringe communities was much greater than in the mid-size central city. As suggested by others (Bountress, 1983), the urban students may experience less daily and routine exposure to SAE, influencing the levels of SAE produced. In support of this interpretation, we have found that the extent to which students spontaneously produce AAE features is greater in urban-fringe communities (Craig & Washington, 2004a; Thompson et al., 2004). To the extent that exposure to SAE is required to foster bidialectalism, it is not surprising that the students living in the urban-fringe communities with the higher proportions of African Americans are also the students producing the most AAE features. Whereas considerable concern about the Black–White Achievement Gap has emerged in the large urban settings across the country, amounts of AAE may be playing a contributing role. This issue is revisited in chapter 7.

Why have all of the child participants in our research program been speakers of AAE? In sum, a number of factors may be responsible. These factors range from the ways we recruit and sample the language of our participants, to demographic and ethnic motivations within our participating communities for retaining one's status as a speaker of AAE. These potential influences are important considerations for any researcher in determining whether a student is a speaker of AAE.

QUANTIFYING OVERALL FEATURE PRODUCTION

In order to help characterize the distributional characteristics of child AAE, we developed a new measure (Craig et al., 1998a), the *dialect density measure* (DDM). The motivation for developing the DDM was driven by a need to quantify and characterize the wide variations in numbers of features produced across students, in a context where an appropriate mathematical base for the calculation was unknown.

Calculation of *percent produced in obligatory contexts* is the more traditional approach to characterizing the development of morphology (Brown, 1973) and would be the logical first choice for characterizing the African American child's acquisition of the feature system. However, the state of our knowledge regarding the linguistic environments in which AAE features are produced remains too limited to determine in which linguistic contexts the AAE feature is optional versus required. When features are characterized by optional inclusion or exclusion rules, it is unclear whether producing or not producing the form is the standard for specific sentence environments. Is production or nonproduction appropriate/obligatory when a student says: *He sick* and *She is hurt*. Are both appropriate, and therefore are both obligatory contexts even though the formulation varies? Do both contribute to any base for calculation and analysis purposes?

When quantifying feature production, it is problematic to assume that the second formulation in the example above: *She is hurt*, is the one that is noncontrastive with SAE, and thus the base in any formulation. This emphasizes inclusion over exclusion and that may yield an incomplete and even inaccurate understanding of the rules governing certain AAE features. At this time, therefore, most attempts at adopting *percent obligatory context* as a base are premature. Again, it is problematic to simply apply rules characterizing adult competence. Conceivably, developmental stages would allow for differences from adults and this should impact consequent calculations. Clearly many questions remain and must be answered before this traditional approach to quantifying morphology can be applied to AAE-speaking students.

The reader is directed to important work being done in the search for rules governing contrastive and noncontrastive productions of morphological forms produced by children that are part of mature AAE feature systems. Some of the work of Seymour and his colleagues focuses on identifying the constraints or rules governing contrastive feature production, for example negative concord (Coles-White, 2004), and copula inclusion and exclusion (Wyatt, 1996). Cumulative information across child features, necessary to evaluate the dialectal system as a whole, remains forthcoming.

In our earliest work, we reported frequencies of feature production as a percentage of the utterances containing at least one AAE feature (Craig & Washington, 1994; Washington & Craig, 1994). Accordingly, if 10% of a student's utterances included one AAE feature, and 10% included two or more, then in both cases 20% of that child's utterances were calculated as amounts of AAE. If the student was a preschooler, then the utterances were relatively short, and multiple AAE features per utterance were infrequent. Accordingly, this was a fairly faithful representation of the distribution of AAE across the discourse of very young students. However, features can and do occur in multiples resulting in more than one AAE feature per C-unit, especially for older students who produce longer utterances. For example, in the following C-unit, the student produced two instances of the copula/ auxiliary deletion of the verb *to be* and one instance of multiple negation, so three AAE features were used.

he _ gonna fall 'cause he _ skating <u>without no</u> leg

As we began to work with older students, this utterance-based calculation became less satisfactory on a conceptual basis. Utterance lengths increased with grade. During free play, the average C-unit length in words for 4-year-olds was 3.14 and for 6-year-olds was 3.81, a statistically significant increase (Craig et al., 1998a). Using the percentage of utterances containing one or more features resulted in the same values for a child who produced one feature in every utterance and a child who produced more than one feature in every utterance. This seemed likely to underestimate dialect production at older ages.

Alternatively, the DDM calculation divides the number of features by the number of words in a sample and yields a rate of feature production in words. Rate measures, however, have their own limitations. Both the numerator and denominator will correlate so the interaction between the two variables may be what is changing. Although this has potential to be difficult to interpret when the focus of inquiry is rate relative to specific features, conceptually this should be less of a problem when rate is the point, as it has been for our distributional analyses. The DDM has been fruitful in analyses of AAE at all ages and, as discussed in later chapters, has revealed important relationships between DDM rates and other language and literacy skills.

SOURCES OF SYSTEMATIC VARIATION IN DDM

A number of systematic sources of rate variation were apparent in the discourse of our African American students, and these are discussed next.

Grade and DDMs

Perhaps the most dramatic systematic variation in DDMs was observed relative to grade level. Most notably, two steep decreases in dialect production rates occurred between preschool and fifth grade. In other words, across the elementary grades, AAE-speaking students increasingly adopted the SAE of the classroom.

The first dialect shift occurred at first grade. In Craig and Washington (2004a), we examined distributions by grade of the morpho-syntactic features of AAE produced during our picture description task. Whereas the phonological feature system has not been applied to the preschoolers and kindergartners, the figure displays DDMs calculated using only the morpho-syntactic feature system (MorDDMs). Figure 5.1 displays the DDM relationships relative to grade based on data reported by Craig and Washington (2004a). As can be seen in the figure, the DDMs for first through fifth grade present a relatively flat distribution. The DDMs also were not different at a statistical level between preschool and kindergarten. However, the preschoolers/kindergartners produced significantly higher feature production rates than the first through fifth graders. At school entry the youngest students in our samples produced features at a level approximately twice that of the students in the elementary grades. In other words, MorDDMs de-

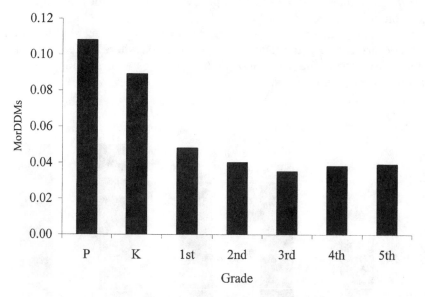

FIG. 5.1. MorDDMs by grade. From "Grade-Related Changes in the Production of African American English," by H. K. Craig and J. A. Washington, 2004, *Journal of Speech, Language, and Hearing Research, 47*, p. 454. Copyright 2004 by the American Speech-Language-Hearing Association. Reprinted with permission.

creased from approximately one morpho-syntactic feature for every 10 words in preschool and kindergarten to only one morpho-syntactic feature for every approximately 26 words from first grade on. As is discussed in chapter 9, this dialect shifting to SAE is associated with positive academic achievements.

Although MorDDMs represented a stable value after the shift at first grade, the number of different types actually increased (Craig & Washington, 2004a). In order to explore the types of features produced relative to grade level, we examined only those features produced by 25% or more of the participants at each grade. The 25% criterion was an arbitrary cut-off but was adopted to de-emphasize the rarer features and characterize what was more typical for the population as a whole. Using a 25% disbursement criterion, the first graders used three different morpho-syntactic types, the second and third graders used six, and the fourth and fifth graders used eight different types. Figure 5.2 depicts these relationships. As a whole, the data indicate that the students were using a larger repertoire of morpho-syntactic features, but less frequently, as they progressed through the elementary grades.

A different pattern was observable for the phonological feature system. For the phonological features, the same five types were produced at comparable levels regardless of grade. These included *g*-dropping, substitution for *th*, consonant cluster reduction, post-vocalic consonant reduction, and syllable deletion.

In summary, these data indicate that a downward dialect shift for child AAE occurs at first grade. This occurs in a context where students are producing essentially the same phonological features across grades, but are acquiring more morpho-syntactic features.

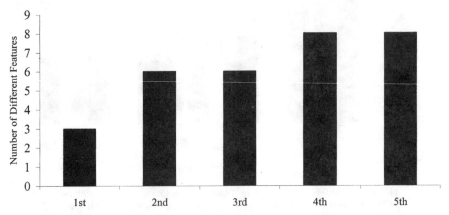

FIG. 5.2. The mean number of different morpho-syntactic features produced by 25% or more of the students at each grade.

The second dialect shift was observed at third grade. As reported in Craig, Thompson, et al. (2003), we examined total DDMs based on all feature systems: morpho-syntactic, phonological, and combination child AAE features, for second through fifth graders in the context of oral reading. We began with second graders because our interest was focused on the reading of text. Whereas all participants were elementary grade students, the examination of phonological features was possible as well as the morpho-syntactic ones. We found that total DDMs decreased significantly by grade in the reading context, as presented in Fig. 5.3. The second graders produced significantly more AAE, approximately three times more than third, fourth, and fifth graders. However, after Grade 2, the DDMs were not significantly different from each other.

The decrease at third grade seemed due to a decrease in phonological feature production. The phonological DDM and combination DDM subsystems (Craig, Thompson, et al., 2003) showed decreases at Grade 3 that mirrored the distributions for the Total DDMs. Again the magnitude of the differences for the phonological features was two to three times greater for second grade compared to Grades 3, 4, and 5. The morpho-syntactic DDMs were low, and were not significantly different by grade for the reading context.

In summary, AAE production changes significantly across the early school years. Two periods for dialect shifting occur during the early elementary grades, one at first grade for spoken discourse and one at third grade for oral reading. The first shift substantially reduces the production of morpho-syntactic features and the second shift substantially reduces the production of phonological features. The timing of these shifts appears to be triggered by important schooling influences. The first shift appears to be

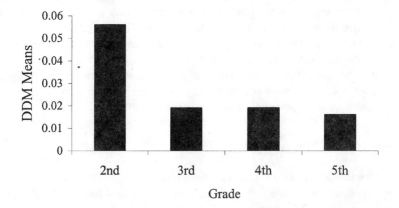

FIG. 5.3. Total DDMs while reading aloud, by grade. Data from "Performance of Elementary-Grade African American Students on the Gray Oral Reading Tests," by H. K. Craig, C. A. Thompson, J. A. Washington, and S. L. Potter, 2004, *Language, Speech, and Hearing Services in Schools, 35*, p. 347.

triggered by immersion in the language of the classroom whereas the second appears to be influenced by formal reading instruction.

Spoken dialect shifting during picture description at first grade is early in the process of participating in full days of MCE classrooms and the MCE curriculum. Dialect shifting for reading at third grade is relatively early in the process of reading acquisition, at the instructional juncture between an emphasis on decoding and one on comprehension.

Pragmatic models of child language acquisition are suggestive that spoken linguistic form is dependent upon discourse context, and that part of language acquisition is learning to match form to function (Bates & MacWhinney, 1989; Craig, 1995; Ninio & Snow, 1999). It is not surprising, therefore, that many African American students become sensitive to the SAE and more formal MCE demands of classrooms and texts, are responsive to these formal exposures, and begin to adapt their linguistic forms to these linguistic contexts in relatively short timeframes.

Who dialect shifts? There is some evidence in our data that it is the students who are the most linguistically advanced. First, the MorDDMs, a measure of tokens, decreased across grades. Older children with more schooling produced fewer AAE features than younger students. Decreased rates occurred in conjunction with a steady increase in types. Knowing more dialect features likely results from being more advanced cognitively and linguistically, knowing more about language in general, and thus is evidence of greater linguistic knowledge. Advancing grade is associated, therefore, both with dialect shifting and with larger feature sets.

A second source of evidence to support this hypothesis that dialect shifting relates to greater linguistic skill derives from PPVT–III scores of the same students (Craig & Washington, 2004a). Higher PPVT–III scores presumably reflect greater vocabulary knowledge. Thus the higher PPVT–III scores of the dialect shifters are consistent with this interpretation that the dialect shifters are the more linguistically advanced students. Although it was not possible to determine a causal relationship in this investigation, intuitively it seems possible that the more linguistically advanced students are the ones who also are pragmatically sensitive and able to accomplish dialect shifting spontaneously from exposure to MCE classrooms.

Socioeconomic Status, Gender, and DDM

Outcomes for DDMs relative to SES and gender have evidenced a mixed relationship over the course of our research program. When we first looked at these variables (Washington & Craig, 1998), we examined the free play samples of 66 kindergartners. As we observed in Washington and Craig (1998), boys are overrepresented on the special education caseloads of public schools across the nation. If dialectal variations are misinterpreted as signs of language disorders, then boys, and students from LSES homes, may be high risk for misidentification. Appendix C summarizes this information. At that time in our research program, we had not yet created the DDM. Amounts of dialect produced by the kindergartners in the Washington and Craig (1998) report was based on tokens, or raw frequencies of feature production, produced within free play samples of consistent length (i.e., 50 C-units).

The second time we examined these variables, 400 preschool through fifth graders participated, the data collection context was picture description, and the amount of feature production was calculated using DDMs (Craig & Washington, 2004a). No statistically significant relationships were found between the DDMs and either SES or gender. Appendix C summarizes these nonsignificant relationships.

Considered together, our research indicates that although dialect production levels are greater for boys and for children from LSES homes at the time of school entry, these effects disappear across the elementary grades. Participation in formal schooling seems to level these early effects. It will be important for future research to determine the intersection between SES, gender, and as discussed next—community, on the extent to which young students produce AAE features so that their heritage language is well understood by teachers and clinicians evaluating their language acquisition skills at the time they enter school. In addition, teachers and clinicians would benefit from knowing more precisely which aspects of formal schooling minimize the dialect differences between boys and girls, and students from LSES and MSES homes.

Community and DDM

Students from two communities in southeastern Lower Michigan have been the primary participants in our research program. As discussed in chapter 3, approximately 75% of our students resided in an urban-fringe community in Michigan. The remainder resided in a mid-size central city in Michigan, which is a college town.

These two communities are similar in many ways. A major difference between the communities, however, is that the percentage of African American students enrolled in the urban-fringe community's public schools is 86% whereas in the mid-size central city the percentage is 16% (Standard & Poor's School Evaluation Services). Students in the urban-fringe community, therefore, live in a community where the dominant culture is African American. By implication, the urban-fringe students are immersed in AAE as part of the cultural–linguistic environment in which they live, whereas the mid-size central students are more likely to experience SAE on a regular and more frequent basis by virtue of the demographics of their community.

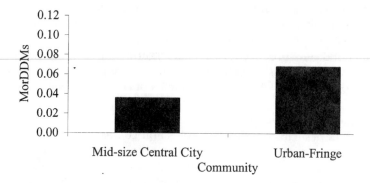

FIG. 5.4. MorDDMs by community. From "Grade-Related Changes in the Production of African American English," by H. K. Craig and J. A. Washington, 2004, *Journal of Speech, Language, and Hearing Research, 47*, p. 454. Copyright 2004 by the American Speech-Language-Hearing Association. Reprinted with permission.

Figure 5.4 depicts the differences in the dialect production rates of the students in the two communities. Morpho-syntactic feature production for the students in the urban-fringe community occurs at approximately twice the rate of that for the students in the mid-size central city. This occurred in a context where other linguistic skills were comparable (Thompson et al., 2004). Immersion in one's own cultural–linguistic community, therefore, relates to higher rates of feature production but not other aspects of oral language performances. The impact of community may be circumscribed to dialectal differences. However, whereas dialectal competence and the acquisition of bidialectal skills influences reading and vocabulary (Craig & Washington, 2004a), it will be important to improve our understanding of the role of community and the core subcomponent variables that constitute community influences on outcomes for African American students.

Language Production Context and DDM

Discourse genre influences the amounts of feature production by African American students. We have compared language production during free play and picture description (Washington et al., 1998), and among picture description, reading SAE text aloud, and writing (Thompson et al., 2004). DDMs varied at statistically significant levels across contexts.

We found that picture description elicits more instances and a greater variety of features than free play (Washington et al., 1998). The participants were 4- to 6-year-olds, and the measures were tokens and types of morpho-syntactic AAE produced within 50 C-unit language samples. Appendix C summarizes this information.

In addition, when we examined the AAE produced by 50 typically developing African American third graders, we found that all produced AAE during picture description, and most produced AAE during reading (92%) and writing (62%). However, DDMs were significantly lower in the two literacy contexts compared to picture description (Thompson et al., 2004). Appendix C summarizes this information.

SUMMARY

Child AAE feature production rates vary in interesting and systematic ways. Our findings for the distributional characteristics of child AAE can be summarized as follows. Production rates for AAE features decrease with increases in grade. With longer systematic exposure to SAE, on average students reduce the frequency with which they use AAE features in school contexts. This is manifested as a dialect shift at first grade for spoken discourse and at third grade for reading aloud. DDMs are an effective way to detect systematic differences in dialect production rates. DDMs underscore the importance of conceiving of young African American students as speakers of AAE rather than as producers of isolated features. In addition to grade, SES and gender relate to AAE production rates at the time of school entry. Language production context and community influence AAE rates across the early grades.

6

NONDIALECTAL EXPRESSIVE AND RECEPTIVE LANGUAGE SKILLS

The importance of understanding a child's oral language skills is not debatable. A variety of practitioners depend on knowing whether oral language development is progressing according to normal expectations or whether there is evidence of a delay or disorder. Strong language skills are foundational to literacy acquisition, academic achievement, and social competence. Unfortunately, the paucity of information regarding the language development of African American children has been a major barrier to improving our understanding of their academic successes and failures.

In our research program, therefore, a priority has been to characterize the nondialectal skills of typically developing African American students, those aspects of oral language that are not AAE feature based. This goal has been pursued in parallel with studies of the dialectal features characterizing their discourse. Although dialectal and nondialectal language behaviors are distinguishable, they must be considered in concert in order to fully understand the AAE-speaking student.

This chapter discusses findings for a set of traditional measures of language that we selected for in-depth study. They take the form of standardized tests, language sampling analyses, and tasks designed to create opportunities for specific types of responding. Additional discussion and scoring details are presented in Appendix D.

The following sections are organized in terms of expressive and receptive language skills. This is an artificial distinction to some extent because expressive and receptive language skills are interdependent. Expressive language tests require that the student has comprehended the instructions and understood the language concepts involved. Similarly, many measures of language comprehension depend on expressive language skills for their responses.

EXPRESSIVE LANGUAGE SKILLS

This section reports outcomes for expressive language measures derived from child-centered oral language sampling—average formulation-unit lengths, amounts of complex syntax, lexical diversity, and performance on a formal test—the Expressive Vocabulary Test (EVT, Williams, 1997). Measures of these types are long-standing in the language assessment literature and are very familiar; thus clinicians require no special training for their implementation with African American students. Furthermore, scoring and interpretation are not dependent upon understanding the child's use of AAE, no matter how preferable a more complete knowledge of the dialect might be. Values are reported on these traditional measures in Appendix D to make available a quantified set of expectations for African American students rather than relying on estimates derived from the study of SAE-speaking students.

Our early work on nondialectal aspects of language, those that are not feature based, focused exclusively on the skills of preschoolers and kindergartners, and elicited samples of their language production during free play with toys. More recently, as we have addressed language and literacy relationships, and as we have learned more about the influence of different types of discourse genre on child AAE production rates, we have adopted picture descriptions as the primary language-sampling context. Accordingly, we have been able to examine language formulation skills across grades, controlling for context.

Preschoolers and kindergartners were not different from each other in the average length of their picture descriptions (M = 22.1 and 19.6 C-units, respectively). However, an increase occurred at third grade (M = 27.2 C-units). This level of C-unit production per picture description then remained constant through fifth grade. These picture description samples were the basis for the observations made throughout this section on expressive language skills.

Mean Length of C-units (MLCU)

Average formulation-unit length is an important and well-established quantitative metric of language development (Brown, 1973; Scott, 1988), used both for clinical evaluation purposes, and for creating language-similar peer matches for research purposes. For SAE-speaking children, measures of formulation-unit length have taken a variety of forms. These measures reflect

either morpheme or word counts as the numerator, and sentences, utterances, or clause-defined units as the denominator. Calculations of mean
number of words per sentence (MLR, McCarthy, 1930; Templin, 1957) or
morphemes per utterance (MLU, Brown, 1973; Miller, 1981; Scarborough,
Wyckoff, & Davidson, 1986) may be the two most widely used approaches.
Morphemes and words per terminable units (T-units, Hunt, 1970; Klecan-
Aker & Hedrick, 1985), and C-units (C-units, Loban, 1976; Miller, 1991) have
been important measures as well, especially for older students and for literacy contexts.

For SAE speakers, formulation-unit length increases with age and grade
(Hunt, 1970; Klecan-Aker & Hedrick, 1985; Miller, 1991) although the spans
for detecting change increase as students become older (Scott, 1988). At
early ages, formulation-unit lengths are associated with increasing grammatical complexity (Brown, 1973; Scarborough et al., 1986) but at older ages
this relationship is less clear (Miller, 1991). Beyond approximately 4 years
of age, the measures become contextually sensitive and reliabilities are
harder to establish (Klee & Fitzgerald, 1985; Kramer, James, & Saxman, 1979;
Scarborough et al., 1986).

Early in our research program, we realized that the lack of information
on child AAE features represented a major challenge to characterizing even
the nondialectal aspects of the oral language skills of African American students. Measures of early language growth, in particular those counting morphemes such as MLU-based calculations, were difficult to interpret because
so much is unknown about optionality in the acquisition of child AAE. The
omission of morphemes occurs within many AAE features, such as variations in subject–verb agreement (*all the boy_ falling down*), and these have
the potential to lower MLU values compared to when the forms are included. For a child whose discourse is densely marked with AAE features,
the MLU might be lower than expected based on SAE derived values, potentially influencing in a negative way the practitioner's assessment of the African American child's sentence structure skills. In the following example, it
is apparent that any morpheme-based count gives the SAE speaker an advantage.

AAE speaker: everybody keep skating 'cause they slippery.
                (8 morphemes; 2 clauses)
SAE speaker: everybody keeps skating 'cause they are slippery.
                (10 morphemes; 2 clauses)

In the absence of critical information about child AAE, our solution to
this problem was to avoid traditional measures of formulation-unit length
that depended upon morphemes as the unit of analysis. As presented in
chapter 4, 29 of the 40 types of features used by participants in our research

program included morpheme variations, and their frequencies of occurrence could impact any morpheme count. Alternatively, we have calculated MLCUs based on words. Only 13 of the 40 child AAE features in our scoring taxonomy operate at a word level, including features which both add words (double copula/auxiliary/modal: *I'm is the girl*) as well as subtract words (copula forms of *to be*: *he _ goin' home*) compared to comparable sentences in SAE. A word-based calculation, therefore, offers a more conservative approach to estimating average C-unit lengths.

We found that statistically significant grade differences characterized C-unit production lengths. As Craig et al. (in press) observed, MLCUs were not statistically different from the immediately preceding or following grade. However, MLCUs increased significantly when more than one grade span was examined. For example, the MLCUs of first graders (M = 6.02 words) were significantly longer than those of preschoolers (M = 4.38). They were significantly shorter than those produced by third graders (M = 6.99). They were not statistically different from those of the kindergartners or second graders. Considered together, our data for African American students corresponded closely to the existing information available for SAE speakers. Formulation-unit length increased with age and grade although the spans for detecting change increased as students become older.

Gender differences were apparent on this measure. The MLCUs of the girls were slightly greater (M = 6.5) than the boys (M = 6.2).

Amounts of Complex Syntax (Csyn)

The acquisition of complex syntactic structures is a major achievement of early childhood, and failure to acquire complex syntax is a robust indicator of a language disorder (Aram & Nation, 1975; Leonard, 1972; Menyuk, 1964; Stark & Tallal, 1981; Watkins, 1994). Understanding teachers' questions in classrooms and formulating appropriate responses are important skills for school success (Loban, 1976; Tyack & Ingram, 1977). In addition, text comprehension depends in critical ways upon a sound knowledge of complex syntax (Bowey, 1986; Demont & Gombert, 1996), and more advanced syntactic skills at school entry predict later third-grade reading comprehension scores (Craig, Connor, & Washington, 2003).

Using an etic–emic approach as described in chapter 4, our complex syntax codes were first identified by searching transcripts for structures described in the extant literature for mainstream children. Sources included: Bloom and Lahey (1978), Brown (1973), Miller (1981), Fletcher and Garman (1988), and Owens (1988). The complex syntax taxonomy included early-developing forms such as *infinitives with same subject* (e.g., *the girl tried to catch him*) and ranged to later-developing *subordination* (expressing temporal relationships: *when it snows you should ice skate*) and *relative clauses* (e.g., *and she's telling the girl that can skate real good to come on*). The most frequent types of complex syntax for the youngest students were those that had shared referents and that avoided breaking up subject–verb relationships or rearranging sentence elements, for example: *infinitive with same subject* (*but he's starting to fall*), *coordinate conjunctions* (*and he's slipping and falling*). The students in the later grades more frequently produced subject–verb relationships that broke up main clauses and rearranged sentence elements (e.g., *the man that was driving the car is really mad*) (Craig & Washington, 1994; Craig et al., in press). Appendix E provides the resulting taxonomy for scoring complex syntax.

In the emic phase of this analysis, we were able to examine distributional relationships related to grade, gender, and SES. Statistically significant grade differences were apparent. These differences were between nonconsecutive rather than consecutive grades. For example, the fifth graders produced significantly more complex syntax ($M = .82$) than the third graders ($M = .64$), who produced significantly more complex syntax than the first graders ($M = .45$), who in turn produced significantly more than the preschoolers ($M = .24$). Overall, the complex syntactic structures described for mainstream children were applicable to African American students as well.

Performances also varied systematically on this measure relative to gender. The Csyn for the girls were slightly greater ($M = .58$) than the boys ($M = .50$). Performances on Csyn did not vary significantly by SES during the school years.

Number of Different Words (NDW)

The number of different words produced in a language sample is another longstanding measure of oral language (Miller, 1981; Templin, 1957) used to estimate lexical diversity. It is a simple frequency count of the vocabulary items produced by the student. NDW is a fairly sensitive measure and plays a useful role in a language assessment battery for both SAE and AAE speakers (Craig & Washington, 2000; Miller, 1996; Thompson, 2003; Watkins, Kelly, Harbers, & Hollis, 1995).

NDW does not control for opportunity, so it is important to use the same corpus size when comparisons are being made to the performances of others. Watkins et al. (1995) compared NDWs using sample sizes of 50- and 100- utterance samples and 100- and 200- word samples and found that preschoolers with specific language impairment and their MLU-matched peers produced significantly fewer different words than their age-matched peers. We have based our calculations on 50 C-unit samples (Craig & Washington, 2000; Craig et al., in press). An alternative to controlling corpus sizes is to calculate Type-Token Ratios (TTRs). TTRs are calculated by using the number of different words value as the numerator, and then by dividing the total number of words produced in the same sample. Unfortunately, TTRs do not distinguish between the lexical expressions of students from different SES backgrounds or gender (Richards, 1987; Templin, 1957). Furthermore, they are not different for students presenting language impairments from those with typically developing language (Watkins et al., 1995). Overall, TTRs seem less informative than NDWs in fixed sample sizes.

Like MLCU and Csyn, NDW varied significantly by grade and again these differences were between nonconsecutive grades for our preschoolers through fifth graders. For example, the NDWs were greater for the fifth graders (3.78) than the third graders (3.37) than the kindergartners (2.77).

Expressive Vocabulary

As the agenda within our research program has grown, we have added more tasks to our data collection protocol. One of these is the Expressive Vocabulary Test (EVT, Williams, 1997). The EVT was added to our protocol because it is co-normed with the Peabody Picture Vocabulary Test–III (PPVT–III, Dunn & Dunn, 1997), one of the most frequently used vocabulary instruments. Co-norming between these two instruments allows for direct comparisons between expressive and receptive vocabulary skill.

Prior research has demonstrated that expressive vocabulary skills are more highly correlated to school performance than receptive vocabulary skills (Scarborough, 1998), and expressive vocabulary skills may be of particular importance to children with poor language abilities (Gray, Plante, Vance, & Henrichsen, 1999). Additionally, it has been suggested that African American students have an oral language preference and performance advantage (Champion, 2003; Champion, Seymour, & Camarata, 1995; Heath, 1983), making the expressive vocabulary skills of this population all the more important to understand.

We have examined the appropriateness of the EVT for use with African American students, and found it informative for characterizing the lexical skills of preschoolers and kindergartners (Thomas-Tate, Washington, Craig, & Packard, 2005) and fourth graders (Thompson, 2003). In both studies, mean scores on the EVT approximated the expected standard score mean of 100 (preschoolers and kindergartners: $M = 98.53$; fourth graders: $M = 97.0$), with appropriate statistical performance spread. Behavioral data gathered from any relatively homogeneous sample of students should evidence considerable performance spread on the measure. Some students should excel, others should perform poorly, and most students should perform within a middle or average range. Our data indicated that the EVT had these characteristics and, therefore, we recommend the EVT for vocabulary testing with African American students.

RECEPTIVE LANGUAGE SKILLS

Any characterization of oral language skills would be critically incomplete without complementary description of the student's comprehension skills. Comprehension skills are important to becoming a competent participant in conversational interactions. In addition, good comprehension skills allow the child to internalize, interpret, and categorize meanings from the world around and to cognitively build mental models of this increasing knowledge (Golinkoff & Hirsh-Pasek, 1995). In order to contribute to this important line of research, our research program has examined comprehension of vocabulary and syntactic–semantic structures, as discussed next.

Receptive Vocabulary

The Peabody Picture Vocabulary Test–Third Edition (PPVT–III, Dunn & Dunn, 1997) is one of the most widely used tests of language, and has been a part of evaluation protocols developed for both clinical and research purposes since the original version was published in 1959 (Dunn, 1959). Unfortunately, as a measure of a student's breadth of vocabulary knowledge, the two earliest versions discriminated against African American students (Washington & Craig, 1992). A major revision, published as the third edition of the test, is much improved. The PPVT–III reexamined the stimulus items used in the second version of the test, the PPVT–R (Dunn & Dunn, 1981), and eliminated 75 items that seemed discriminatory based on race/ethnicity (Williams & Wang, 1997). Although Stockman (2000) acknowledged the validity of the PPVT–III for use with this population, she questioned whether the standardization changes made to the PPVT–III really addressed bias, and advised continued caution in its interpretation.

We examined the PPVT–III for appropriateness as a measure of vocabulary performance for at-risk African American preschoolers and found that the PPVT–III fared well (Washington & Craig, 1999). Unlike the PPVT–R, the PPVT–III yielded a performance spread that approximated the normal distribution. All of the students in this investigation were considered at risk, and the performance mean for the group was lower than hoped, albeit not unexpected given their at-risk status. Their mean score on the PPVT–III was 91, compared to the standardization mean of 100. Although still well within the normal performance range, these scores were best characterized as low average.

Of interest, the PPVT–III detected a difference in the vocabulary scores of the students relative to the educational level of their primary caregivers. Again, compared to a standardization mean of 100, the mean PPVT–III standard scores for preschoolers whose primary caregiver had attained high school graduation ($M = 93$) or better ($M = 94$) were significantly greater than the preschoolers whose caregiver had not matriculated from high school ($M = 77$). Overall, the PPVT–III appeared both appropriate and informative for the assessment of the vocabulary skills of African American students, and we continue to use it as part of our evaluation protocol (see chapter 7 for additional discussion).

Whereas the PPVT–III is now administered as a standard part of our evaluation protocol, we have new data for another 235 students (72 LSES, 163 MSES), this time in first through fifth grades, and this is reported in Appendix D. Like the outcomes for younger African American children reported in our earlier work (Washington & Craig, 1999), children of college graduates perform significantly better ($M = 103$) on this test than students whose caregivers have only high school ($M = 96$) or less than high school ($M = 93$) educational levels.

Responses to Wh-Questions (Wh-q)

Appropriate responding to questions is acquired developmentally (Chapman, 1988; Craig et al., 1998b; Parnell, Patterson, & Harding, 1984). Connected speech sampling is a limited and often ambiguous context in which to assess a student's understanding of questions. Some questions have a low probability of occurrence in natural discourse and must be elicited in other ways. Accordingly, we developed an elicitation task designed to probe a student's ability to respond to a fairly large set of question types that varied in terms of cognitive demand and syntactic sentence forms (Craig et al., 1998b; Washington & Craig, 2002). Examples include: "What he doin," "Where this," "Which kids are going (action)," and "Why she (action) here."

The task presents two colored action pictures; one depicted a snow-shoveling scene and the second depicted a beach scene. The scoring system assigns full credit when the student produces the target response, and partial credit when the response reflects understanding of the question's intent but is factually inaccurate. Less partial credit is assigned for responses that reflect understanding that a request for information has been presented but the concept underlying the specific type of information requested has not been understood.

We have found that preschool through fifth grader performances increased steadily with grade on the Wh-q task. For example, preschoolers produced significantly fewer correct responses than all of the other grades. Kindergartners produced significantly more correct responses than preschoolers, and significantly fewer correct responses than first graders. First graders produced significantly more correct responses than both the kindergartners and preschoolers and significantly fewer correct responses than the grades above them. The second through fifth graders produced significantly more correct responses than the preschoolers through first graders. Another grade difference was observed between Grades 2 and 5, but not the grades in between these. Overall, although correct responding continued to increase after second grade, the span of grades necessary to detect significant increases in performance became quite large.

Responses to Reversible Sentence Probes of the Active/ Passive Voice Distinction (RevS)

This task explored children's word order strategies for comprehension of the distinction between active and passive sentence constructions. Students who are SAE speakers comprehend active sentence constructions in the form of agent-action-patient (e.g., *Bobby hugged Susie*), using word order cues, at around 4 years of age (Beilin & Sack, 1975; Bever, 1970; Chapman, 1988; Fraser, Bellugi, & Brown, 1963; Maratsos, Kuczaj, Fox, & Chalkley, 1979). Passive sentence constructions are later developing (e.g., *Susie was hugged by Bobby*), and SAE-speaking 4-year-olds may confuse active and passive sentence constructions.

We used reversible sentence probes, a well-established approach to oral language comprehension (Roberts, 1983), to explore the word order comprehension strategies of young AAE-speaking students ages 4 to 7 years (Craig et al., 1998b). Students were presented with a forced choice picture-pointing task, another longstanding and informative approach to the assessment of oral language with young children (Fraser et al., 1963), and asked to point to the picture that went with what the examiner said. Figure 6.1 presents an example of the picture pairs used in this task. Three sentence prompts were spoken by the examiner for each of 10 pairs of pictures. The sentence prompts included two active voice trials and one passive voice trial. The prompts that correspond to the pictures in Fig. 6.1 are the following:

The dog chase the cat.	Target Active Voice Trial
The cat chase the dog.	Foil Active Voice Trial
The cat was chased by the dog.	Passive Trial

The scoring of the RevS task only assigned a response to the passive voice prompt as correct if the student also responded correctly to the active voice prompt. Details of this scoring process are provided in Appendix D.

RevS showed steadily increasing performance scores with grade from preschool through second grade. Statistically, the grade effects were significant. Preschoolers had fewer correct responses than any of the other grades. Kindergartners had more correct responses than preschoolers, but fewer than the other grades, and first graders had fewer correct responses

FIG. 6.1. One of the pairs of pictures used to present two probes of the active voice and one of the passive voice distinction. From "Reversible Sentences Task," by H. K. Craig and J. A. Washington, 2001. Copyright 2001 by The Regents of the University of Michigan.

than second through fifth graders. As reported by Craig et al. (in press), after Grade 2, the values remained essentially the same, around 18.5 points out of a potential total score of 20, with decreasing variation in scores within each grade that was suggestive of a ceiling effect. By the end of second grade, most typically developing African American students comprehend the active/passive voice distinction in sentences.

SUMMARY

Malik's oral language skills evidenced considerable growth across the elementary grades. As presented in Table 1.1 in the first chapter of this book, at fourth grade, his MLCU, Csyn, RevS, and Wh-q scores all were appreciably higher than at school entry. However, only his score on the Wh-q task met expectations for his grade. His expressive and receptive language skills had grown, but had not achieved the levels of his peers.

This chapter discussed data from a set of studies designed to characterize the expressive and receptive language skills of typically developing African American students, from preschool through fifth grade. A number of traditional approaches to characterizing language growth have proved informative and appropriate for African American students. Values for these measures are provided in Appendix D to provide a set of performance expectations for typically developing African American students on each. All of these measures clearly demonstrate that the trajectory for growth for African American students' expressive and receptive language skills is the same as has been observed for SAE students. Language change for young children is rapid, such that considerable growth can be detected within short developmental time spans. As language matures, observable growth slows, and becomes detectable across longer time periods. As can be seen in the next chapter, these measures contribute in important ways to a comprehensive language evaluation battery suitable for African American elementary-grade students.

7

EVALUATING LANGUAGE
AT SCHOOL ENTRY

This chapter presents a model for evaluating the language skills of African American students. The *Michigan Protocol for African American Language* (MPAL) has been developed from the work of our research program over the last decade and represents the reevaluation of time-tested traditional approaches for their appropriateness with African American students. This chapter begins with a brief background orientation to the issues involved in developing culture-fair evaluations for African American students, and then presents the MPAL model.

BACKGROUND

Historically, African American students have been at considerable risk for being misidentified as language disordered because of a dearth of culturally fair language evaluation instruments. Culturally appropriate evaluation protocols must be able to distinguish the typical from the atypical African American language learner. Prior to the turn of this century, nondiscriminatory language tests for African American students were simply not available, and two types of testing errors were the frequent result. African American students who were developing language normally were at risk for being wrongly identified as language disordered, and African American students with true language problems might not have been identified and therefore would not have received needed intervention services.

Two approaches were attempted in the past to try to address the need for nondiscriminatory tests. The two alternatives included renorming established tests, and providing scoring credits for items on standardized instruments that were potentially impacted by AAE. The success of these approaches varied based on whether the test was an articulation or a language test. Haynes and Moran (1989) renormed the Sounds-in-Words subtest of the Goldman-Fristoe Test of Articulation (Goldman & Fristoe, 1986). This renorming was successful for accommodating a small set of features of AAE that were phonological in nature. Cole and Taylor (1990) modified the scoring of three well-known articulation tests, the Templin-Darley Tests of Articulation, Second Edition (Templin & Darley, 1969), the Arizona Articulation Proficiency Scale–Revised (Fudala, 1974), and the Photo Articulation Test (Pendergast, Dickey, Selmar, & Soder, 1969). The scoring adjustments improved performances, as well as the face validity of each instrument. These methods offered a way to significantly reduce false clinical diagnoses of articulation impairment in students who spoke AAE.

However, changes to established language tests did not improve their appropriateness for use with African American students in the same way that the modification of articulation tests had done. In some cases, notably the Test of Language Development (TOLD, Newcomer & Hammill, 1977), performances by African American students were so low that renorming or scoring adjustments were not possible (Wiener, Lewnau, & Erway, 1983). The Peabody Picture Vocabulary Test and the Peabody Picture Vocabulary Test–Revised (PPVT, Dunn, 1959; PPVT–R, Dunn & Dunn, 1981) were similarly problematic. Although the PPVT–R included African American students in the standardization sample, preschoolers and kindergartners failed to perform as expected (Washington & Craig, 1994). Most children performed more than one standard deviation below the standard score mean of 100. Crediting 16 different items missed by at least half of the students failed to improve the performance distributions appreciably. In contrast, the Peabody Picture Vocabulary Test–Third Edition (PPVT–III, Dunn & Dunn, 1997) fared much better. This third edition included more African American students in its standardization sample, improved the pictured stimulus set, and disaggregated the data by race and ethnicity to ensure comparability. In our research program, we have found this version of the test to be informative for preschoolers through fifth graders (Washington & Craig, 1999; see chapter 6 of this volume).

There are lessons to be learned from these attempts at updating established tests to make them more culturally and linguistically fair. First, articulation is more amenable to this process than language. Second, simply including a small number of African American children in the normative sample without considering performance differences that may characterize specific racial and ethnic groups will not necessarily yield a culturally fair test. Third, the preponderance of African American students performing at the low end of a test's statistical distribution of scores, with little performance spread across children, does not achieve the statistical requirement for a good test. Statistically, tests must approximate a normal performance curve. Otherwise, the performance of an individual child cannot be compared statistically with normal expectations for his or her own culture. In the absence of appropriate tests, and in a national context where formal testing is increasingly required, overidentification of African American children for language and learning problems remains a concern.

THE MPAL MODEL

Although many African American students produce features of AAE at the time of school entry, major aspects of their discourse do not reflect the operation of these dialectal forms. AAE forms are incorporated into fewer than 20% of the words of even the heaviest feature producers at the time of kindergarten (Washington et al., 1998), and these levels decrease further during the elementary grades (Craig & Washington, 2004a). Early in our research program (Craig, 1996; Craig & Washington, 1994), we proposed that as information on child AAE is gathered, we cannot and need not wait to develop informative and culturally fair assessment instruments. Accordingly, a major focus of the last decade of research has been to develop assessment strategies for young children that do not depend on our knowledge of AAE feature use by focusing on the nondialectal components of their discourse.

Our model for evaluation, consistent with prevailing views of child language evaluation (ASHA, 2003; Berko-Gleason, 2001; Owens, 2001), is comprised of three major components: screening for a language problem, identification of a language problem, and assessment of language skills. The model is built upon the following assumptions:

1. *The presence of a language disorder can be determined from evaluation of the nondialectal aspects of the African American student's oral language.* The evaluation literature in speech–language pathology is rich in sensitive and informative evaluation procedures. Our research program has devoted considerable effort to determining whether some of the major methods are appropriate for use with African American students. As discussed in the previous chapter, a number of major approaches to language evaluation and analysis lend themselves to the assessment of the nondialectal aspects of the language of African American students who speak AAE. These approaches employ scoring units that are larger than the phoneme or morpheme and thus avoid the influence of morpho-syntactic and phonological features of child AAE on the performance outcomes. For example, approaches that employ scoring units that are at the level of the whole word

or C-unit detect language growth in typically developing AAE-speaking students, and also distinguish those with language disorders. The methods we have examined are time-tested traditional approaches to language evaluation. They were developed for mainstream students but are also appropriate for African American students because they are not dialect dependent.

2. *All selected instruments are fair and appropriate for use with the target population.* This foundational requirement ensures that the performances of an individual student are being compared to peers. Accordingly, there must be a match between the instrument and the student in terms of the age/grade targets of the instrument and the cultural–linguistic composition of the comparison group. In the past, meeting this requirement has been particularly problematic when evaluating the language and literacy skills of African American students.

3. *Both expressive and receptive language skills must be evaluated.* Any assessment of language that focuses only on production or only on comprehension will be critically incomplete. It can be especially challenging to find formal methods to assess expressive language skills if the student's comprehension skills are weak. For example, if the student does not comprehend the sentence spoken by the examiner, then even responding to expressive tasks like elicited imitation may be compromised for that student.

4. *Both formal and informal methods should be involved.* Formal methods, known as "tests," are tasks that are supported statistically by standardization data. Formal tests are critical for identifying the presence or absence of a language impairment. In most settings, quantitative reports of performances that are supported by normative statements are required for documentation purposes, and are the basis for determining whether a student does or does not qualify for special services. Particularly in school settings, standardization data are required for use in all components of the language evaluation process: screening, identification, and assessment.

Even in settings where formal methods are required, informal methods can complement formal methods, especially in the assessment phase of an evaluation. Informal methods, also known as nonstandardized criterion-referenced tasks, permit profiling of a child's strengths and weaknesses. Using informal methods, the clinician may adopt a strict criterion in which a student is expected to demonstrate a particular skill by a specified age or grade. An example of applying a strict criterion to student performance would be the expectation that a student would comprehend the active/passive voice distinction if he or she were a first or second grader (Craig et al., in press). Criterion-referenced methods also include the category of tasks that represent traditional approaches to assessment, but which are characterized by less comprehensive statistical support, and may depend on normative expectations generated at a local level. An example of applying a locally generated norm would be the expectation that a second-grade student enrolled in the Metropolitan Detroit, Michigan public schools would produce C-unit lengths of approximately 8 words on average (Craig et al., in press). This local normative expectation can then be interpreted in the context of standards outside of the child's school district or even compared to a national standard. For example, 8 words per C-unit is a recognized standard for second graders based on the work of Loban (1976).

5. *Measurement techniques should evaluate growth.* Improvement should be assessed in terms of increases in performances over time as well as progress toward an established standard or expectation for performance on the behavior of interest. Both aspects of tracking language changes are important. For example, over the course of a school year, a child should show growth in oral language behaviors such as average sentence length, but also should show progress toward the expectation for that language behavior, such as production of a particular average sentence length for his or her grade. Measurement must evaluate both progress over time *and* attainment of the standard.

6. *Language performances will be interpreted in the context of information about the student's hearing and cognitive status.* Basic to any identification of a language disorder is differential diagnosis. Knowing the student's auditory and cognitive status are two key components to this determination.

7. *Each skill should be evaluated more than once.* Determination of strengths and weaknesses should not rest upon a single score. Prior to identifying the presence of a language problem, or difficulty with a specific component skill, more than one measurement should be made. Repeated difficulties across tasks can then be used to confirm that the original low performance was a valid indication of a language disorder. Repeated measurements reduce potential sampling errors so that a student is not misdiagnosed as language disordered when the poor performance might be attributable to other factors. There are many reasons why a student might perform below expectations on a particular instrument. Fatigue and/or disinterest are potential factors that may result in false impressions of a student's abilities. Furthermore, the particular performance may reflect a very circumscribed deficit resulting from a problem with one specific skill rather than a more general language disorder.

8. *Strengths and weaknesses should be evaluated in ecologically valid contexts.* Ecologically valid contexts for assessing a student's language skills

are those that are authentic. For students, tasks that assess language in contexts that are comparable to those encountered in classrooms will have high ecological validity. Classroom language demands are many and varied. Can the student respond to oral directions? Ask and answer questions? Provide descriptive and narrative discourse?

9. *The clinician possesses competencies in dialectal knowledge, culture-fair instruments, and culturally and linguistically appropriate adaptations of assessments.* Effective evaluation depends on a knowledgeable clinician. Currently, clinicians have the advantage of tremendous amounts of new information about the language and literacy skills of African American students to support the evaluation process that were not available even a decade ago. Clinician knowledge should include familiarity with the features of the major dialects of American English and how these features might impact the child's performance on the language instruments used for evaluation. This requires that the clinician examine instruments of choice and audit and alter them for appropriateness with the local linguistic community. Although determination of a language disorder does not require assessment of the student's AAE, it is important that the clinician be knowledgeable about its characteristics. Knowledge of this type will be particularly important when clinicians target linguistic problems as goals for intervention. Intervention goals should address morpho-syntactic or phonological forms of disorder, not features of dialect.

The three components of the MPAL model are presented in Fig. 7.1. The Protocol includes repeated measures of both receptive and expressive skills, evaluations across the major language domains, and both formal and informal methods. There is no one-on-one relationship between the type of method and its function within the Protocol, with the exception that tests are required to meet the purposes of the Identification Phase. Otherwise, both formal and informal methods are used to screen and assess specific sets of skills. The MPAL model was developed to assess language, and represents a set of processes to complete the language portion of an evaluation with African American students. A comprehensive speech–language evaluation will need to include an oral–motor examination, and supplemental measures appropriate to the child's specific needs, for example reports from teacher interviews and classroom observations. Each phase of the MPAL process is discussed next.

The Screening Phase

Why is the Screening Phase important? Valid and reliable screenings both eliminate from further testing those children whose speech and language skills are developmentally appropriate, and identify children who need ad-

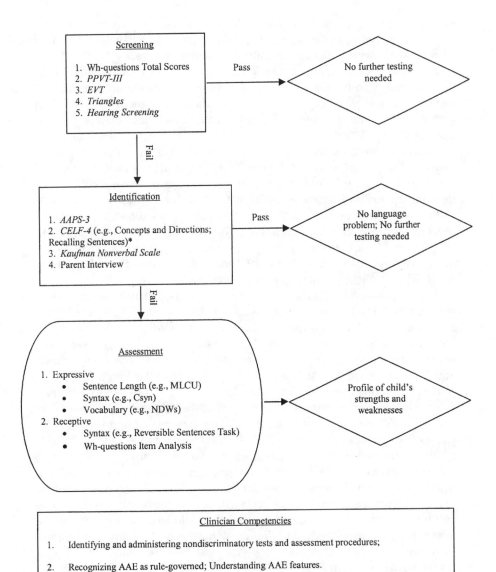

FIG. 7.1. The language evaluation model recommended for African American students based on our research outcomes. (The formal methods are italicized and the informal methods are not.) *Note:* CELF–P (Recalling Sentences in Context, Linguistic Concepts) for 4-year-olds.

ditional language assessment. As can be seen in Fig. 7.1, one outcome of a successful screening is to find children who pass the screening. Children who pass the screening likely require no further service.

As shown in Fig. 7.1, the other outcome of a successful screening is to find children who fail the screening. A good screening should overidentify rather than underidentify students for further assessment consideration without identifying so many false positives that caseloads become overburdened (Klee et al., 2000; Law et al., 2000). Some of these students who do not perform well on the screening will later be determined to have normal language abilities during the Identification Phase of the evaluation process. However, the larger group of students who fail the screening will later be determined to have language problems. All children who have language skills below the expected range should be reliably identified in the screening. Furthermore, information derived from the screening can be added to that gathered during other parts of the evaluation process to provide a more comprehensive description of the student's speech and language skills, while avoiding unnecessary redundancy.

Among children who have language problems, not surprisingly, the more severe manifestations are easiest to detect (Law et al., 2000; Westerlund & Sundelin, 2000). The data for African American children suggest that this trend may be true cross-culturally. In our research program, we have developed a screening protocol that successfully meets key screening criteria and is appropriate for African American students (Washington & Craig, 2004). At this time, we have only tested its validity and reliability with preschoolers and kindergartners. However, a number of the components of the Protocol have been evaluated separately and fare well at first through fifth grades (Craig et al., 1998b; Craig et al., in press; Craig & Washington, 2000).

By virtue of disproportionate representation in low-income homes, cross-generational literacy limitations, and the impact of dialect, African American students in many communities are high risk for language difficulties. We recommend that they be screened at the time of school entry using culturally appropriate screening instruments. Indeed, whereas oral language skills are foundational to literacy acquisition and academic achievement, we recommend that every high-risk student be screened at school entry regardless of race or ethnicity. Now that appropriate screening instruments are available for young African American students, for some communities more universal screening can become a reality.

Components of the Screening Protocol. The MPAL Screening Protocol is comprised of five components: the total scores on the Wh-questions task (Wh-q), the PPVT–III, the EVT, the Triangles subtest of the K–ABC, and a hearing screening. These particular tasks were selected because as a set they have a brief administration time, approximately 20 minutes, and they are informative (Washington & Craig, 2004). The Screening Protocol includes formal tests to meet the requirements of schools for formal test scores for documentation purposes. Although we first included a language sample collection as part of the Screening Protocol, the information gained from it in the form of MLCU was not informative. The performances of students on the Wh-questions and PPVT–III tasks, in contrast, were highly predictive of performances on a larger assessment (Washington & Craig, 2004).

The Wh-questions task was developed in two stages. We first reported outcomes on this task just for preschoolers and kindergartners (Craig et al., 1998b; Craig & Washington, 2002). More recently, we have reported outcomes for first through fifth graders (Craig et al., in press). In order to use this task with students in Grades 1 to 5, we added seven additional, cognitively more challenging probes to the original twelve. (See chapter 6 for further discussion of this measure). The Wh-q task plays an important role in the Screening Phase of the MPAL, and thus needs to be as brief as possible. Accordingly, we examined the response profiles of all of the first to fifth graders who have participated in our research program in the past, and searched for which prompts elicited full credit responses (3 points) on both pictures for most students (89%–90% of students) at each grade. These are provided in Appendix F. They can be considered optional in order to shorten administration time.

The EVT provides a standardized expressive language measure, an important component of language screenings and assessments. Although not a part of our assessment battery in the past (Craig & Washington, 2002), we now use this test consistently as part of the Screening Phase and find it informative (Washington & Craig, 2004). The Wh-questions task and the PPVT–III are discussed in more detail in chapter 6.

The Identification Phase

Why is the Identification Phase important? Most screenings overidentify some children who upon further evaluation are determined to have no language deficits. Misclassification based on inappropriate interpretation of cultural interaction and communication styles may contribute to difficulty with detection of true language problems for minority students (Chamberlain & Madeiros-Landurand, 1991). The Identification Phase provides additional testing time for students who have not passed the Screening to determine whether a language disorder is indeed present.

Two case examples are presented to demonstrate the ways in which the Screening and subsequent Identification and Assessment Phases of the MPAL can work together. The following case example illustrates a true fail. Markeya, a low-income African American girl, 48 months of age, demonstrated average IQ on both the screening and the full Kaufman Nonverbal

TABLE 7.1
Screening and Assessment Scores for Markeya, an African
American Preschool Girl From a Low-Income Home

Screening Instrument	Obtained Score	Expected Scores	
		Mean (SD)	Range
Triangles	12	10 (3)	7–13
Wh-Questions	46	53.2 (5.3)	47.9–58.5
PPVT–III	72	100 (15)	85–115
Identification and Assessment Instruments			
KNVS	102	100 (15)	85–115
MLCU (50 C-units)	2.44	3.15 (.72)	2.43–3.87
Csyn	0	4.3 (3.2)	1.1–7.5
NDW (for females)	59	79.5 (14.8)	64.7–94.3
RevS	5	12.3 (3.8)	8.5–16.1
NRT (% phonemes correct)	73.4	82.4 (9.5)	72.9–91.9
AAPS–3	89	100 (15)	85–115

Note. PPVT–III (Peabody Picture Vocabulary Test, 3rd ed), KNVS (Kaufman Nonverbal Scale), MLCU (Mean Length C-Unit), Csyn (Complex Syntax), NDW (Number of Different Words), RevS (Reversible Sentences), NRT (Nonword Repetition Task), AAPS–3 (Arizona Articulation Proficiency Scale, 3rd ed.) Expected Scores from Craig & Washington, 2002; Washington & Craig, 2004.

Scale for cognition (see Table 7.1). However, she showed poor language performance overall on both the Screening and the follow-up Identification and Assessment instruments: reduced utterance lengths, below average vocabulary (−1.25 *SD* below the mean), no evidence of complex syntax, and poor phonological working memory skills (NRT). Markeya is a true fail and is classified as SLI based on her normal cognition, poor language ability, and absence of any additional etiological factors (hearing loss, motor disturbance, etc.).

Tyrik, a low-income African American boy, 51 months of age, performed poorly on the Screening measures, as shown in Table 7.2, resulting in a *fail* classification. However, follow-up administration of the full Assessment revealed average to above average language skills in most areas for Tyrik. On the basis of a screening alone, his low scores on Triangles and PPVT–III would have led to his misclassification as language impaired. Although not all identification and assessment instruments were administered to this child, further available testing indicated that his nonverbal (KNVS) and comprehension (RevS) scores were within the expected ranges.

If a clinician terminates the evaluation with the Identification Phase completed, the following important question can be answered: Does this student present a language problem? The answer to this question will determine the student's eligibility for special services and is basic to appropriate case management. Termination of the evaluation process at the Identifica-

TABLE 7.2
Screening and Assessment Scores for Tyrik, an African
American Preschool Boy From a Low-Income Home

Screening Instrument	Obtained Score	Expected Scores	
		Mean (SD)	Range
Triangles	5	10 (3)	7–13
Wh-Questions	48	53.2 (5.3)	47.9–58.5
PPVT–III	77	100 (15)	85–115
Identification and Assessment Instruments			
KNVS	102	100 (15)	85–115
MLCU (50 C-units)	3.42	3.15 (.72)	2.43–3.87
Csyn	7	4.3 (3.2)	1.1–7.5
NDW (for males)	71	70.6 (16.5)	54.1–87.1
RevS	16	12.3 (3.8)	8.5–16.1
NRT (% phonemes correct)	87.7	82.4 (9.5)	72.9–91.9
AAPS–3	94.5	100 (15)	85–115

Note. PPVT–III (Peabody Picture Vocabulary Test, 3rd ed), KNVS (Kaufman Nonverbal Scale), MLCU (Mean Length C-Unit), Csyn (Complex Syntax), NDW (Number of Different Words), RevS (Reversible Sentences), NRT (Nonword Repetition Task), AAPS–3 (Arizona Articulation Proficiency Scale, 3rd ed.)

tion Phase will not allow the clinician to answer another important question: What is this student's profile of strengths and weaknesses? Completion of the Assessment Phase of the MPAL evaluation will provide answers to this question, and is discussed later in this chapter.

Components of the Identification Protocol. The Identification Protocol includes the AAPS–3, CELF–4, the remainder of the Kaufman Nonverbal Scale, and a Parent Interview. Together these tests and interview instrument build on the standardized tests that are part of the Screening Phase. They meet the assumptions for an appropriate battery discussed earlier in this chapter, in that they are culture-fair, permit more than one look at receptive and expressive language skills in contributing to a diagnosis of language impairment, and the contexts are ecologically valid.

The AAPS–2 provides an appropriate evaluation of the articulation skills of African American students without penalty for the phonological features of AAE. Washington and Craig (1992) demonstrated that this test was informative when distinguishing students with poor articulation skills from those with good articulation skills without scoring adjustments for their use of dialect. Cole and Taylor (1990) provide a scoring adjustment system appropriate for students who are speakers of Southern AAE.

The Concepts and Directions subtest of the CELF–4 provides an appropriate evaluation of a student's ability to follow multistep oral directions.

The Recalling Sentences subtest of the CELF–4 requires the student to re-peat sentences of increasing syntactic complexity and length. Both of these types of skills are particularly valuable in a classroom context. Thompson (2003) found that the same subtests from the CELF–3 distinguished the lan-guage skills of typically developing African American students who differed in reading proficiency. Students who were proficient readers scored signifi-cantly higher on both subtests than students who were struggling readers.

We recommend the Triangles subtest of the K–ABC as part of the Screening Phase of the MPAL. We recommend the remaining subtests com-prising the Kaufman Nonverbal Scale to be used as part of the Identification Phase. Use of a nonverbal scale for evaluation of cognitive skills does not penalize students who are linguistically different or have language disor-ders. Information about cognitive function in general as well as a profile of important cognitive skills is key information to facilitate the interpretation of language outcomes, and for profiling learning styles. The K–ABC includes a representative sample of African American students and students with language disorders in the standardization sample.

Appendix G provides the reader with a copy of the parent question-naire we have developed for use in our research program. It yields impor-tant information about the socioeconomic background and educational history of the family, the child's educational, medical, and developmental history, and behavior. At this time, when most of what is known about typ-ical African American families and socialization practices is scant, this questionnaire was designed to provide the clinician with potentially im-portant information to again support planning for the evaluation. It may be informative for the clinician to know about the family's history of lan-guage, learning and reading difficulties, including information about the student's own experience with books. Information of this type will impact interpretation of poor reading performances. The student who has had lit-tle exposure to books outside of the classroom may benefit from a broad based instructional program that increases reading opportunities, whereas a student who has reading difficulties despite extensive exposure may need a specific focus on early reading skills such as understanding pho-neme–grapheme correspondences.

In using information gained from a parent questionnaire, it is important that the clinician avoid using family patterns as an excuse for a student's failure. Frequently we hear teachers comment on the family of a struggling African American reader, saying something like: "well you know his mother can't read either." Low family literacy levels indeed may be part of the ex-planation for a student's failure to achieve basic reading levels, but this does not remove our educational and clinical responsibilities to ensure that that student learns to read.

The Assessment Phase

Why is the Assessment Phase important? Once a student has been identified as having a language disorder, it is important to profile linguistic strengths and weaknesses. These profiles support the writing of goal statements for intervention. Combined with information gathered from measures in the Screening and Identification Phases, performance on the assessment measures should provide a fairly comprehensive description of the expressive and receptive skills, which are weak, as well as those that are strong enough to support intervention efforts directed at the problem skill sets.

Components of the Assessment Phase. Our research program has revealed that many fairly traditional approaches can be used to profile the oral language strengths and weaknesses of elementary-grade African American students. This same insight appears to undergird the structure and composition of most of the DELV (Seymour et al., 2003). A major advantage to the use of traditional assessment measures like those in MPAL and the DELV is that their application and interpretation require no special training for speech–language pathologists. Clinicians will readily recognize and already be using these or similar tasks to assess the language skills of any student who qualifies for enrollment on their caseloads.

The MPAL assessment strategies have been primarily criterion-referenced in nature. Whereas standardized tests meet the identification function of the evaluation protocol, our assessment tasks did not need to provide this type of information and could be more descriptive and qualitative rather than quantitative. However, we have attempted to provide quantitative statements to support each task so that a set of expectations for typical performance, primary to assessing a child's skill level as average, above, or below average, were available for clinical purposes. These are provided in the Appendixes supplementing chapter 6. These values allow the clinician to compare the performance of any individual student to the criteria for expected performance established for each task, and thus develop targeted interventions as appropriate.

MPAL creates a profile of oral language strengths and weaknesses. As can be seen in Fig. 7.1, three of the measures tap expressive and two receptive language skills. Spoken vocabulary diversity is assessed, and syntax is evaluated twice, once in the expressive and once in the receptive modality. In addition, MLCU in words provides a quick measure of average sentence length, and an item analysis of the responses to Wh-q tasks reveals which types of requests for information the student comprehends and which he or she does not.

The following case examples illustrate how the scores from the assessment may be used to develop a comprehensive profile of elementary-grade African American students. Two first-grade students, La Toya (female) and Demarcus (male) were assessed using MPAL. Both students lived in the same urban-fringe community and were from middle-SES backgrounds. La Toya demonstrated weak receptive compared to expressive language skills (see Table 7.3). La Toya's performances on the language measures indicate that she likely will have difficulty comprehending instructions and tasks with demanding vocabulary. In contrast, Demarcus demonstrated strong language skills (see Table 7.3), did not fail the screening, and was chosen for comparison purposes. His language profile suggests that he likely will have minimal difficulty understanding and using language to engage in classroom discourse and to learn academic subjects when compared to his typically developing peers. Comprehensive language profiles such as these should enable teachers and clinicians to develop and provide appropriate classroom instruction and support for elementary-grade African American students.

Determining Dialect Status. The presence or absence of AAE forms in an African American child's repertoire significantly affects the clinician's assessment choices. Our evaluation protocol is appropriate for any African American child whether the child speaks SAE or AAE. However, the African American child who speaks SAE has other evaluation instruments available as well. Presumably, African American children who speak SAE present no special challenge for the speech–language pathologist (SLP) in terms of either evaluation or intervention. Since these children are not speakers of AAE, standardized testing instruments that at least include African Americans in the normative sample should be informative and appropriate for

TABLE 7.3
Language Profiles of Two MSES Elementary-Grade African
American Students from an Urban-Fringe Community

Measure	Female with low language skills	Male with average language skills	Expected Score Range
Triangles	12	10	7–13
PPVT–III	83	124	85–115
RevS	14	18	17.0–20.4[a]
Wh-q	93	108	94.1–106.5[a]
MLCU	5.17	5.50	4.8–7.2[a]
Csyn	.39	.92	.21–.69[a]
NDW	2.7	3.8	2.4–3.6[a]

[a]Expected scores from "Oral Language Expectations for African American Children in Grades 1 Through 5," by H. K. Craig, J. A. Washington, and C. A. Thompson, in press.

them. Obviously the clinician will want to be cognizant and respectful of the child's cultural heritage in making many decisions around evaluation and intervention tasks and activities, as is the case when planning for all clients.

If an African American student is not clearly a speaker of SAE, however, the clinician faces a number of challenges in planning an appropriate assessment. The clinician must determine whether the student's oral language performances are consistent with AAE, or reflect the presence of a language disorder. The American Speech-Language-Hearing Association (ASHA) provides guidelines for clinicians evaluating students who speak American English dialects, and states the following:

Difference versus Disorder

A speaker of any language or dialect may exhibit a language disorder unrelated to his or her use of the native dialect. An essential step toward making accurate assessments of communication disorders is to distinguish between those aspects of linguistic variation that represent regular patterns in the speaker's dialect and those that represent true disorders in speech and language. (*ASHA Supplement* 23, in press, p. 2)

It is important not to assume that because a child is racially Black, he or she is a speaker of AAE. Table 7.4 provides a real example of an interaction that occurred between a well-meaning but misinformed clinician and an African American parent. The interaction demonstrates the kinds of misunderstandings that can result when clinicians do not recognize social dialects and make faulty assumptions about African American students and their dialect status.

Our data (Craig & Washington, 2004a; Washington & Craig, 1994) indicate that many African American students will evidence zero copula/auxiliary (*it time to eat*), zero article (*this cake is (the) best present of all*), and variable subject–verb agreement (*and the kids is going across the street*) in their discourse. Unfortunately, these variations from SAE characterize language disorders in mainstream students. As discussed in chapter 4, it is not yet clear whether some of these patterns, particularly those related to verb tense marking, also serve as clinical markers for language disorder cross-culturally. Consequently, in the absence of clear-cut guidelines, the clinician must ask: Are these variations from SAE evidence of a dialect or part of a disorder pattern, or is it not possible to make this determination?

There are two approaches available currently to determine the dialect status of an African American child. One approach is to use the single available published test designed to determine whether a child is an AAE speaker or not. Seymour et al. (2003) have recently published the Diagnostic Evaluation of Language Variation (DELV), a package of tests that comprehensively approach diagnostic evaluations and are consistent with our

TABLE 7.4

An Example of a Serious Misinterpretation of

ASHA's Guidelines on Treatment of Social Dialects

Jalen is a 5-year-old African American child who lives in a mid-size central city in the Midwest. Jalen has an older brother and both parents are highly educated. Jalen was referred to the speech–language clinician for help with sentence structure and morphology. Jalen was not a speaker of AAE.

Clinician	Parent
I want to take some time Mrs. M. to review the speech and language goals I have decided to set for Jalen's therapy.	
	Ok.
Jalen is not producing several language structures that we would expect at this age. For example, when he tries to say more than one idea in a sentence, he omits the conjunction.	
	Yes I have noticed that. And also I notice that when he produces sentences he omits verbs. So he might say: He sitting down instead of He is sitting down. Will you be working on that also?
No. Deleting verbs like <u>is</u> and <u>are</u> represent normal dialect variations for children who speak African American English. Sometimes the children include the verb and sometimes they don't and both are ok.	
	What?
You know, AAE is a dialect that African American children use and the American Speech and Hearing Association says I shouldn't treat it, because it's not a disorder.	
	But Jalen is not a dialect user. None of his family speak AAE. I think it is part of his language disorder. And, he always omits those verb forms, this isn't some kind of choice on his part.
Oh no Mrs. M. it's dialect. This is a very common feature of AAE.	

model for evaluating the language skills of African American students. Part 1 of the DELV Screening test is designed to determine the child's language variation status. The examiner prompts while pointing at stimuli, "I see little kites. I see a big kite. The boys have little kites, but the girl ..." (have/ got, has, something else, no response). To target the 3rd person do/does form, the following prompt is given: "This boy likes to play basketball, but this girl ..." (don't, doesn't, something else, no response). As more information about the differences between disorder and dialect accumulates, clinicians will be better equipped to decide whether this test is informative for students in their communities.

An alternative approach involves scoring the student's discourse for AAE in real time, as part of a short conversation. This is the method that we use in our research program and in applied contexts within schools. In brief conversation with the student, the clinician can listen for the presence of selected forms, and record their occurrence using a checklist. We recommend that the examiner listen for forms consistent with the morpho-syntactic features of child AAE rather than phonological features prior to first grade. After first grade an AAE speaker will likely produce the g-dropping feature (Craig, Thompson, et al., 2003) and the examiner may listen for this feature as well. Students who use AAE morpho-syntactic forms may also be using phonological forms, but we have found that phonological features of AAE are not likely to be used alone (Craig, Thompson, et al., 2003; Craig & Washington, 2004a). Asking the student to describe an action picture is a quick and easy way to elicit a sample of spoken discourse that will likely include these three or four AAE features if the child is an AAE speaker. Appendix H presents a checklist the reader may use when listening for features.

Two outcomes are possible using the checklist, as follows:

1. Variations from expected behaviors *are not* consistent with AAE features but overlap with errors characteristic of language disorder.
2. Variations from expected behaviors *are* consistent with AAE features but overlap with errors characteristic of language disorder.

The first outcome suggests that the student is not likely a speaker of AAE and instruments developed for SAE speakers may be appropriate for assessment purposes with that child. The clinician then may serve as a valuable resource to the student's teachers by helping others understand that although the student is African American, the variations from SAE are not consistent with spoken AAE. The second outcome will require intensive investigation of potential assessment instruments by the clinician and is important to understand if morpho-syntactic or phonological goals will be addressed during intervention.

SUMMARY

Malik's language skills were evaluated at preschool and again at fourth grade (see chapter 1, Table 1.1). His performance profile demonstrates the ways in which many of the instruments discussed in this chapter can provide useful information about an African American student's language skills. His standardized testing revealed intact cognitive skills, but a low average performance score on the PPVT–III. Malik's only skill area that was comparable to the mean scores of his peers was responses to requests for information. In contrast, assessment of his expressive language skills revealed shorter than average C-unit lengths and less complex syntax than that of his peers. He did not understand the difference between active and passive sentence structures. Although Malik was not diagnosed as language disordered, his oral language skills were generally weak.

This chapter discussed the need for nondiscriminatory and informative evaluation instruments appropriate to the language skills of African American students like Malik. The *Michigan Protocol for African American Language* (MPAL) is presented and discussed in terms of its theoretical model and assumptions, the components of the three phases of MPAL, and examples of ways in which the protocol can be applied to educational and clinical contexts.

AFRICAN AMERICAN CHILDREN IN ACADEMIC DISTRESS

Many African American children underachieve or even fail academically. To illustrate this point, Table 8.1 summarizes performances for African American students based on national data from the NAEP, and presents performances in four major content areas relative to White peers for comparison purposes.

The future of our country needs most students to achieve at Proficient levels in these foundational content areas. As we look to today's students to become tomorrow's leaders, the national trends are disheartening overall and appalling for African American students. Most White students demonstrate at least Basic skills at all grades whereas half or fewer of African American students achieve Basic skill levels for reading, science, or math. Writing and fourth-grade math are the exceptions. Most African American students demonstrate Basic level writing skills across grades, but again these numbers are considerably lower than for the White students. At all grades across the country, African American students perform much lower than their White peers, and most African American students fail to achieve Proficient skill levels at any grade in any subject.

What has come to be known as the "Black–White Achievement Gap" has been a problem for a number of decades. Fishback and Baskin (1991) observed that the performance gap was apparent as long ago as 1910. Although substantial improvements in achievement scores have been reported for African American students in recent decades (Hedges & Nowell, 1998; Hoffman & Llagas, 2003) as apparent from Table 8.1, the gap still exists. The gap can be detected early, at the time of school entry, widens across the elementary grades, and persists into high school (Phillips,

TABLE 8.1
Comparisons of Academic Indicators for African American
and White Students in Grades 4, 8, and 12 on the NAEP
for [1]2003, [2]2002, and [3]2000 as Available

Content Area	Grade	% at or Above Skill Level	African American	White
Reading	4th [2]	Proficient	12	41
		Basic	40	75
	8th [2]	Proficient	13	41
		Basic	55	84
	12th [2]	Proficient	16	42
		Basic	54	79
Writing	4th [2]	Proficient	14	34
		Basic	77	90
	8th [2]	Proficient	13	38
		Basic	74	90
	12th [2]	Proficient	9	28
		Basic	59	79
Science	4th[3]	Proficient	7	38
		Basic	34	79
	8th [3]	Proficient	7	41
		Basic	26	74
	12th [3]	Proficient	3	23
		Basic	22	62
Math	4th [1]	Proficient	10	43
		Basic	54	87
	8th [1]	Proficient	7	37
		Basic	39	80
	12th [3]	Proficient	3	20
		Basic	31	74

Note. Proficient represents solid academic performance for each grade assessed. Students reaching this level have demonstrated competency over challenging subject matter, including subject-matter knowledge, application of such knowledge to real-world situations, and analytical skills appropriate to the subject matter. *Basic* denotes partial mastery of prerequisite knowledge and skills that are fundamental for proficient work at each grade. From Braswell, Daane, and Grigg (2003); Braswell, Lutkus, Grigg, Santapau, Tay-Lim, and Johnson (2001); Grigg, Daane, Jin, and Campbell (2003); O'Sullivan, Lauko, Grigg, Qian, and Zhang (2003); Persky, Daane, and Jin (2003).

Crouse, & Ralph, 1998). Today, African American fourth graders are more than twice as likely to perform at the lowest levels on national tests of reading achievement, 60% compared to 25% for their White peers on the NAEP (Grigg et al., 2003). Poor reading skills hinder a student's ability to learn new information from text and thus limits the student's potential to excel in science, math, and geography (Braswell, Daane, & Grigg, 2003; O'Sullivan, Lauko, Grigg, Qian, & Zhang, 2003; Weiss, Lutkus, Hildebrant, & Johnson, 2002). The Gap is observable on many measures of school success including: grade point average, enrollments in special education, enrollments in gifted programs, suspension rates, enrollments in advanced placement classes in high school, high school graduation rates, and rank in high school graduation classes (Artiles & Zamora-Duran, 1997; Harry & Anderson, 1994; Hoffman & Llagas, 2003; Ogbu, 2003; Owings & Magliaro, 1998; Patton, 1998; Russo & Talbert-Johnson, 1997). Post-secondary achievements, in particular college enrollments and percentages of PhD recipients, also appear to be impacted (Hoffer et al., 2003; Hoffman & Llagas, 2003).

This chapter discusses three major hypotheses as to the causes of the Black–White Achievement Gap. Each of these factors has been established in the literature for mainstream students as critical to literacy and thus academic success. Differences from mainstream are usually discussed as risk factors. For example, family socioeconomic status is an important factor in literacy acquisition and academic achievement. MSES or better is associated with positive outcomes, and LSES is an identifiable risk factor. Major risk factors and their contribution to low academic achievement by many African American students are discussed next.

FACTORS CONTRIBUTING TO THE BLACK–WHITE ACHIEVEMENT GAP

No single factor in isolation is responsible for the difficulties that are faced by the African American students who have difficulty achieving academically. Poverty, classroom environments and attitudes to schooling, and early family literacy practices have received considerable attention as potential risk factors for African American students. Each one of these factors is complex, multidimensional, and incompletely understood. For each factor, major findings are reported in the subsequent sections of this chapter.

Poverty

Poverty is one of the most difficult factors to study. Poverty is not an isolated variable, but is better conceptualized as a macro variable that includes the effects of family—especially maternal/caregiver education level, access to resources of many different types ranging from health care, to libraries and museums, to literacy materials, the quality of school environments, opportunities to travel, and on and on.

The role of poverty in the poor academic achievement of many African American students is an extremely important issue because African American children are more than three times as likely as their mainstream peers to live in poverty (Federal Interagency Forum on Child and Family Statistics, FIFCFS, 2003). A considerable amount of the literature on African American students, however, has ignored family socioeconomic status in its research designs, not reporting proportions of students from LSES or MSES homes (see McLoyd, 1991). This is a significant problem when findings between groups are then interpreted as differences between Blacks and Whites, and the importance of the SES differences in explaining these outcomes are not addressed. Much of this research, particularly the earlier studies, therefore, is confounded and uninterpretable.

Even when researchers attempt to control for SES level, for example comparing MSES African American students to MSES White students, or LSES African American students to LSES White students, defining LSES and thus determining which variables must be matched can be very complex. A common variable used to index a family's SES is income. Income alone, however, as a sole index of SES has not been informative as a predictive variable of reading skill levels (Chall et al., 1990). Furthermore, even a fairly objective measure like family income may not tap important differences between groups in the stability of those income levels, accrued savings, or potential inheritances (McLoyd & Ceballo, 1998) so that the financial status of the families may not be as comparable as intended. One outcome of former President Lyndon B. Johnson's "war on poverty" (1964) was establishment of the federal poverty guidelines currently used to qualify individuals for a range of federal and state social services. At best, these guidelines make it possible for poor families to receive much needed benefits, ranging from participation in Head Start to subsidized family housing. At worst, the reliance upon family income to determine poverty status has perpetuated a widespread belief that poverty can be defined simplistically using single variables such as income status. Unlike income, however, caregiver education level is one of the most influential co-variates of SES that is predictive of reading (Chall et al., 1990) and vocabulary (Washington & Craig, 1999). Unfortunately, caregiver education level often is not available to researchers and thus goes unreported, or is embedded in an SES composite variable and its relative contribution not reported separately.

LSES is associated with lower educational levels in the home (Hoffman & Llagas, 2003; McLoyd, 1998). Of special importance for literacy acquisition, children in LSES homes own fewer books. Whereas caregiver reading levels are likely to be low as well, children from LSES homes can be quite limited in their early reading opportunities (Hoffman & Llagas, 2003; Nettles & Perna, 1997). Children from LSES homes need more books, and they need caregivers who can read them well. Additionally, children in poor households are at increased risk for developmental and health problems due to increased exposure to environmental hazards and less access to health care (Brooks-Gunn, Duncan, Klebanov, & Sealand, 1993; Fazio, Naremore, & Connell, 1996). Each of these risks is important in its own right, but considered together for students from LSES homes, places African American students as a group—one of the largest segments of the U.S. population living in poverty—at particular risk for poor academic achievement.

It seems important to improve our understanding of the intrinsic and extrinsic variables that allow some students to achieve despite risk factors compared to peers who also are at risk and fail to achieve. As educators, we must hope that education-based solutions to the potentially profound adverse effects of poverty and its co-variables are possible. Recent research indicates that formal public preschool experience may mitigate some of the deleterious effects of poverty for the acquisition of literacy skills. Craig, Connor, and Washington (2003) followed the reading comprehension growth of two cohorts of African American students observed at Time 1 as either preschoolers or kindergartners. The preschoolers were all LSES, enrolled in a state-funded public preschool for children at risk, whereas the kindergartners were all from MSES homes in the same communities with no public preschool experiences. At first grade, the Time 1 LSES preschoolers were performing as well as the Time 1 MSES kindergartners on the Reading Comprehension portion of the Metropolitan Achievement Tests (MAT–7, 1993), and by second and third grades the Time 1 LSES preschoolers were outperforming the Time 1 MSES kindergartners. By Grade 3, the Time 1 MSES kindergartners evidenced a 1-year lag in performance expectations on the MAT, whereas the Time 1 LSES preschoolers approximated grade level expectations. High-quality early education programs can reduce the negative impact of poverty and its co-variables on later achievement (Barnett, 1995), and this research indicates that their funding must be a national priority.

Other research reveals that at-risk students benefit from prevention programs, which focus on critical early literacy skills (Brown & Felton, 1990; Foorman et al., 1998; Torgesen, 1998; Torgesen et al., 1999; Vellutino et al., 1996; Vellutino, Scanlon, & Tanzman, 1998; Whitehurst et al., 1994). Center-based programs yield positive effects on the cognitive and language skills of young children from LSES homes (Burchinal et al., 2000; Ramey et al., 2000). At the other end of the grade spectrum, Adelman (1999) found that high-quality high school curriculum has a pronounced positive effect on college graduation rates for African American students and these effects are more pronounced than those related to SES. Overall, these studies offer considerable hope for improving the outcomes of the significant numbers of African American children growing up in poverty.

Are the combined effects of LSES and its co-variates a sufficient explanation for the poor academic achievement of those African American students who are part of the Black–White Achievement Gap? Some research indicates that when research designs provide the appropriate controls for race and social class differences, the gap essentially disappears. When children are grouped by SES, racial/ethnic differences in reading skills at school entry are not apparent (Coley, 2002). The reverse, however, is not the case. Large SES differences in achievement exist when children enter school regardless of race (Lee & Burkham, 2002). It appears that at the time of school entry, the Black–White test score gap can be eliminated statistically by controlling a small number of observable characteristics of the students and their environments (children's age, child's birth weight, SES, WIC participation, mother's age at first birth, and number of children's books in the home). Controlling for SES significantly reduces the magnitude of the achievement gap, with estimates that the gap for reading is reduced by more than two thirds, and the gap for math test scores by almost half (Fryer & Levitt, 2002).

> Despite the fact that we see no difference in initial test scores for observationally equivalent Black and White children when they enter kindergarten, their paths diverge once they are in school. Between the beginning of kindergarten and the end of first grade, Black students lose .20 standard deviations relative to White students with similar characteristics. If the gap in test scores for these children continues to grow at the same rate, by fifth grade the Black students will be .50 standard deviations behind their White counterparts—a gap similar in magnitude to that found in previous analyses (Jones et al., 1982; Phillips et al., 1998; Phillips, 2000). (p. 3)

Considered as a whole, this literature indicates that the Black–White Achievement Gap can be explained by SES levels at the time of school entry. It is not surprising that the strongest influences are from home and community prior to schooling, and major differences in SES thereby exert strong influences "at the starting gate" (Lee & Burkham, 2002). However, the gap is not well explained by SES after students are enrolled in formal schooling. The gap grows across grades despite controlling for SES. Accordingly, African American students lose ground compared to their mainstream peers. Fryer and Levitt (2002) found that school quality was uniquely related to growth in the gap, with African American students attending worse schools on average.

Measures of SES, particularly income and parental education, account for no more than one third of the gap between Blacks and Whites (Phillips, Brooks-Gunn, Duncan, Klebanov, & Crane, 1998). Some scholars therefore suggest that poverty is not a sufficient explanation for low achievement, and for reading failure in particular, among African American children. Furthermore, children from low-income homes can demonstrate reading skills at average and at better than average levels (Chall et al., 1990; Thompson & Craig, 2005).

Some of the most recent thought-provoking work on this topic has derived from study of the Black–White Achievement Gap in Shaker Heights, Ohio, an affluent suburb of Cleveland (Ogbu, 2003; Singham, 1998), which boasts one of the best school systems in the nation. Although all students were from

middle to upper-middle class homes, African American students in that community performed lower than their White peers, and this gap was apparent
from elementary grades through high school on a wide range of achievement
measures. African American students from MSES homes outperformed African American students from LSES homes, but the MSES African American
students lagged behind the MSES White students (Ogbu, 2003).

Being raised in an MSES home no more ensures academic success than
being raised in an LSES home prevents it. Accordingly, it will be important
for the planning of prevention and intervention programs appropriate for
African American students to disambiguate the effects of poverty and its co-
variables from other barriers specific to literacy learning. What are the education-based solutions to the disadvantages represented by poverty? How
can African American students from MSES homes improve their performances so that they are reaching their academic potential? By implication,
when the literature on race/SES overlaps are considered as a whole, schools
do a fairly good job of recognizing and understanding the disadvantages
represented by poverty. However, schools do not yet recognize and understand the impact of culture on learning. Research must continue to address
these important questions so educators are equipped with the information
they need to "level the playing field" for all students.

Classroom Environments and Attitudes to Schooling

Early childhood education programs, especially high-quality programs, positively impact children's reading achievement, cognitive skills, behavior,
and potential for referral to special education or for grade retention (Barnett, 1995; Bryant, Peisner-Feinberg, & Clifford, 1993; Campbell & Ramey,
1995; Peisner-Feinberg & Burchinall, 1997). Unfortunately, minority children
and those living in poverty are more likely to participate in early childhood
care and education programs that are low quality (Lee & Burkham, 2002;
Peisner-Feinberg & Burchinal, 1997). As observed by Lee and Burkham,

> Low-SES children begin school at kindergarten in systematically lower-quality
> elementary schools than their more advantaged counterparts. However
> school quality is defined—in terms of higher student achievement, more
> school resources, more qualified teachers, more positive teacher attitudes,
> better neighborhood or school conditions, private vs. public schools—the
> least advantaged U.S. children begin their formal schooling in consistently
> lower-quality schools. This reinforces the inequalities that develop even be-
> fore children reach school age. (p. 2)

The authors go on to say that initial inequalities can be reduced with high-
quality center-based preschool experiences, and by reducing the inequality
of resources within schools.

What are the characteristics of high-quality classrooms? A number of characteristics have been identified in the literature and are important when considering the intractable nature of the Black–White Achievement Gap. Low teacher–student ratios (Biddle & Berliner, 2002; Russell, 1990; Wasley, 2002) characterize high-quality classrooms. Larger class sizes and longer school days decrease the quality of teacher–child interactions, particularly reducing the amount of cognitively challenging talk experienced by the students (Smith & Dickinson, 1994). The frequency and types of teacher–child interactions are basic to classroom quality. Cognitively challenging de-contextualized talk, for example, when the teacher engages students in storytelling using predictions and evaluations as part of book reading, predicts later reading comprehension and vocabulary scores (Dickinson & Smith, 1994).

High-quality teachers teach effectively and effective teachers make a real difference (Darling-Hammond & Youngs, 2002; Singham, 2003). High-quality teachers have higher credentials in terms of degree levels, more years of college education, and more experience in terms of number of years of teaching (Connor, Son, Hindman, & Morrison, 2005; Darling-Hammond & Youngs, 2002). High-quality classrooms also make effective use of paraprofessionals (Schepis, Reid, Ownbey, & Parsons, 2001).

Unfortunately, African American students are more likely than mainstream peers to have poorer quality teachers. Higher percentages of teachers in LSES schools are teaching outside their specialty (Darling-Hammond, 1997). Haycock, Jerald, and Huang (2001) reported that African American eighth graders are more likely than their mainstream peers to have teachers who de-emphasize lab and data analysis skills. African American eighth graders are much less likely to have a certified teacher with subject level competency and more likely to have a teacher who participated only minimally in professional development activities. Haycock et al. (2001) estimated that students of effective teachers outperform students of ineffective teachers at a six-fold level, so these differences in teacher quality have profound implications for African American students and the Black–White Achievement Gap. Singham (2003) proposed that, based on these findings, school systems must develop programmatic approaches to professional development that are sustained, and that provide new teachers with at least 10 years of mentoring, training, and feedback. Whereas African American students are more likely to have beginning teachers or teachers who are less effective, sustained excellent programs of teacher professional development would have a differentially positive effect on African American students and, thereby, should contribute to a narrowing of the achievement gap. Of course this recommendation overlooks the impact of reduced financial resources in poor urban districts. Poor schools in poor school districts may recognize the need for intensive professional development but simply may not be able to deliver these types of support. In poor districts, participation in professional development can be complicated further because the teacher's work is harder so teachers are less available, the pay is poorer so they have fewer of their own resources to devote to these activities, and the budgets are tighter so fewer costs can be compensated or offset at the school or district level.

High teacher expectations characterize high-quality classrooms (Chall et al., 1990; Gill & Reynolds, 1999) and may arm the student against negative influences in the environment (Garmezy, 1991). Alternatively, teachers' low expectations for performance may create a form of self-fulfilling prophecy for African American students. In our own research, we have found that most of the teachers' ratings of African American students are lower than those of parents or the students themselves. Table 8.2 provides examples of some of the questions we have posed, and the comparative responses of approximately 300 teachers, parents, and students.

The reader may be surprised to find the high self-ratings by the students as presented in Table 8.2. A widely held interpretation of the Black–White Achievement Gap is the belief that African American students do not

TABLE 8.2
Mean Values for Ratings of Students' Abilities

Question	Teacher Rating	Parent Rating	Student Rating
How difficult is			
reading?	3.36	3.46	4.00
math?	3.05	2.98	3.74
science?	3.51	3.30	3.96
How difficult are standardized tests?	2.77	2.99	3.65
How likely			
... graduate high school?	4.51	4.80	4.67
... attend college?	3.80	4.40	4.68
Overall classroom performance?	3.14	3.47	4.31

Note. The questions presented to the teachers, parents, and students were worded differently. For example,

> Teacher question: Compared to other children in his/her class, how difficult is reading for this student?
>
> Parent question: Compared to other children in his/her class, how difficult is reading for your child?
>
> Student question: Compared to the kids in your class, how good are you at reading books and papers?

Ratings were made on a 5-point rating scale, where 1 is difficult, unlikely, or poor and 5 is very easy, extremely likely, or excellent. From Craig & Washington (2004c).

achieve like their mainstream peers for fear of "acting White" (Fordham & Ogbu, 1996). Essentially, the hypothesis suggests that achievement is perceived as White so it is devalued and avoided. Ogbu (1992) proposed that whereas African American students grow up in a context where part of the history is one of oppression and discrimination, they develop an identity that is in opposition to the majority culture.

Although this hypothesis is popular, there are strong counterarguments. Spencer, Noll, Stoltzfus, and Harpalani (2001) found an inverse relationship between high Euro-centric racial attitudes and performance on standardized achievement tests. For a large sample of African American youth, followed longitudinally, higher self-esteem and achievement goals were associated with a strong sense of African American identity (Spencer et al., 2001). More recently, Ogbu (2003) characterized the attitudes of African American students in the Shaker Heights community as a "low effort syndrome." Despite recognizing the importance of high achievement, and knowing that they needed to work hard to achieve, the students reported that they "try just enough to get by" (p. 18).

Alternatively, Steele and Aronson (1998) proposed that African American students disconnect from schooling and achievement as a result of "stereotype threat." According to this view, the very students who care the most about high achievement lower their performance levels because they are afraid to try in a climate of negative assumptions about their intellectual abilities. In other words, because the majority culture assumes they cannot achieve, African Americans disconnect so that they "don't" care, rather than "can't" do it. Others suggest that a lack of high achieving African American role models limits the expectations and goals of African American students for themselves, because African American adults are underrepresented in the professional and leadership ranks of students' lives, for example as teachers, administrators, and school board members (Portes, 1996).

The ratings presented in Table 8.2 are consistent with comparisons of students', parents', and teachers' perceptions by other researchers (Ogbu, 2003; Stevenson et al., 1990). As can be seen in Table 8.2, the students' ratings of themselves were high. For example, they rated their overall performance as 4.31 out of 5. In other research, African American students believed in their own academic abilities as much as mainstream peers and generally evidenced high self-regard (Graham, 1994; Willig, Harnisch, Hill, & Maehr, 1983). When elementary-grade African American students were asked to predict how well they would do in high school in reading and mathematics, they were optimistic (Stevenson et al., 1990), and generally enthusiastic about their schoolwork (Ogbu, 2003). They tended to rate themselves as above average in reading and mathematics (Stevenson et al., 1990). African American fifth graders liked reading better than Hispanic and

White children liked reading and both groups of minority children liked homework better than White children liked homework (Stevenson et al., 1990). Similar to White children, African American children believed their parents and their teachers would be pleased with their mathematics and reading performances (Stevenson et al., 1990). African American high school students valued high achievement levels, and evidenced disappointment when achievement was low (Spencer et al., 2001). Furthermore, feelings of popularity were similar among African American students who were high and low achievers; high achievers did not perceive themselves as less popular (Wong & Rowley, 2001). African American students' ratings of their performances were not related to actual achievement (Stevenson et al., 1990), and some students perceived themselves to be doing well when they were not (Ogbu, 2003).

In contrast to their children, African American mothers' ratings correlated with actual achievement (Stevenson et al., 1990). Often, when we lead discussions about the Black–White Test Score Gap, we receive many questions from the audience implying that African American families do not value schooling. This is not the case. The empirical data, as illustrated in Table 8.2 from our own research program, reveals that African American families do value schooling. Similarly, Gutman and McLoyd (2000) found that the caregivers of students from LSES and MSES homes both emphasized the importance of education. Additionally, caregivers recognized that their roles were very important to their child's school success, and again this did not vary by SES. As Wong and Rowley (2001) observed, assumptions that African American families de-value schooling have been based on differences in behaviors and attitudes of students. When parents become the focus of inquiry and are actually asked for their opinions and beliefs, their expectations for their children are high. Similarly, as can be seen in Table 8.2, the parents in our research program set high goals and expect their children to go to college.

Compared to students and their parents, teachers' ratings are lower and correspond better to actual student achievement (Ogbu, 2003; Stevenson et al., 1990). Again, as illustrated in Table 8.2, both student and parent ratings were higher than those of the teachers. Consistent with other researchers, the teacher and parent ratings of our students' abilities correlated significantly to the achievement levels of the students, whereas the students' self-ratings did not. As discussed earlier in the chapter, high-quality teachers can improve the outcomes for disadvantaged students. Furthermore, positive feedback from teachers in the early elementary grades relates to the setting of higher goals by students at the time of high school graduation, and overall better academic success (Slaughter-Defoe & Rubin, 2001). It is also the case that when teachers' expectations for their students increase, student outcomes are higher (Gallimore & Goldenberg, 2001).

Together, the recent studies addressing these issues indicate that African American students rate themselves highly and not very realistically in terms of academic achievement. Teachers rate the students lower than parents or the students themselves, but these teacher evaluations are more consistent with the students' actual achievement levels. As observed by Ogbu (2003), the cause and effect relationships between teacher expectations and student performances are complicated. Despite their importance, as yet these relationships are not very well understood.

Early Family Literacy Practices

A third cluster of factors relate to family literacy practices, which again can be conceptualized as a macro variable, and has received considerable attention from scholars as a potential source for explanations underlying the Black–White Achievement Gap. Family literacy practices, particularly opportunities for home-based storybook reading, are important predictors of later reading skills (Bus, van IJzendoorn, & Pelligrini, 1995; Scarborough & Dobrich, 1994).

As part of the identification with a particular culture, minority families may adopt a different style of literacy practices from mainstream families (Heath, 1983; Ogbu, 1988), and this is the case for many African American families. Daily storybook reading may not be a routine part of the early literacy experiences of African American preschoolers (FIFCFS, 2003), whereas daily reading of storybook texts is a common and early primary form of literacy exposure for mainstream children (DeTemple, 2001; Whitehurst & Lonigan, 2001). Unlike their mainstream peers, African American children may experience print first in environmental forms, such as on food labels, toy trademarks, or signs in their communities. Early exposure to stories for African American students often occurs in the form of oral narratives that are richly descriptive, fictionalized, and often collaborative amongst the adults present (Heath, 1983; Vernon-Feagans, 1996). The African American child's role is to be an attentive listener, a point of contrast to the collaborative question–response routines that characterize mainstream parent–child and preschool teacher–students reading storybooks together (Anderson-Yockel & Haynes, 1994; Feagans & Haskins, 1986; Hammer, 1999; Pelligrini, Perlmutter, Galda, & Brody, 1990).

It seems important to ask whether the young African American student who has considerable knowledge of environmental print faces greater challenges in mastering sound–letter correspondences than the student whose early literacy experiences are centered around text in storybooks. We have raised this question elsewhere (Craig & Washington, 2004b), asking whether the student who is able to name the letters of the alphabet readily, and first learns connections between sounds and letters for highly salient and important family or product names, experiences more difficulty learning conventional spelling rules. For example, how does the African American student sound out words like "smile" and "came" if he or she tries to apply his or her prior knowledge of the spelling of a brother's name: "Davonte" (/dəvɑnte/) and the trademark name: "Nike" (naɪki/)?

Overall, many African American students enter formal schooling with literacy experiences that differ from their mainstream peers, and the mainstream practices are a better fit to early classroom literacy experiences. Literacy practices at home and in school, which are congruent, are advantageous for learning (Barton, 1994; Heath, 1983; Neuman & Roskos, 1992). How can we help bridge home and school practices for African American students in ways that respect heritage cultural practices but prepare the young child for the literacy learning tasks of the classroom? How can teachers work with parents to support these transitions?

NEED FOR A NEW FRAME OF REFERENCE

Malik's school performances mirror many of the problems discussed in this chapter. Of foremost importance, he had difficulty learning to read. When Malik was a second grader and a fourth grader, he was administered the GORT–3, a standardized test of reading. The GORT–3 uses standard scores reported as an Oral Reading Quotient (ORQ). Standard scores equate performances around a mean of 100 with a standard deviation of 15, so at both grades expected performance would be 100, plus or minus 15 points (range 86–114). As a second grader, Malik's reading score (ORQ = 91) was lower than average, but within the acceptable performance range. As a fourth grader, his reading proficiency had fallen (ORQ = 85) compared to expectations so that his skills were only borderline. Poor reading achievement at fourth grade was confirmed on the state achievement test. His Reading MEAP scores fell below the scores necessary to be considered Proficient. Malik's poor reading skills were not an isolated problem. His Math scores on the MEAP, also administered at fourth grade, failed to achieve Proficient levels.

New approaches to understanding students like Malik, and to improving the Black–White achievement gap are needed at this time. The extant literature clearly demonstrates that deficit models, those that compare the skills, abilities, attitudes, and practices of African American students to a mainstream standard have not been fruitful. When mainstream students are held as the standard, and comparisons made to their skills, abilities, attitudes, and practices, the resulting picture can only be a series of similarities or worse, of subtractions.

Both positive and negative aspects of African American students' experiences need to be understood. Some students beat the odds: How do they do this? What are the factors that protect them and foster academic resiliency? Future research should benefit from framing questions and adopting designs that tease apart the confluence of factors that allow some African American children to succeed in the face of adversity sufficient to defeat their peers.

9

RELATIONSHIPS AMONG LANGUAGE AND LITERACY SKILLS FOR AFRICAN AMERICAN STUDENTS

LINKAGES BETWEEN ORAL LANGUAGE AND READING SKILLS

Good oral language skills are foundational to the development of literacy. Whereas African American students lag behind their mainstream peers in the development of reading and this gap is longstanding, the relationships between the language and literacy skills of African American students have been of interest in the past, and again in recent years. Failure to impact the Black–White Achievement Gap in a context of rapid growth in knowledge about the oral language skills of African American students during the last decade has rekindled interest in this line of inquiry. A potential relationship between AAE and reading in particular is receiving renewed attention and is discussed in this chapter. Examples of the influence of AAE on written language samples are presented in the final section.

AAE and Reading

Considerable early research, conducted during the 1970s and 1980s, asked whether there was any evidence of a relationship between AAE and reading for African American students. This question was a logical outgrowth of observations that many African American students have difficulty learning to read, many are speakers of AAE, and language lays the groundwork for reading acquisition. These early studies consistently found that African American students produced AAE while reading aloud, and this was observable across a wide grade span (Rystrom, 1973–1974; Steffensen, Reynolds, McClure, & Guthrie, 1982).

Like the earlier studies, we have found that many of the elementary-grade students participating in our research program produce AAE features while reading aloud passages of SAE text. Craig et al. (2004) reported that 94% of 65 second through fifth graders produced AAE features while reading the SAE text from the GORT–3. Table 9.1 provides a sample of the oral reading of a third-grade African American student participating in our research program. As can be seen in Table 9.1, this student produced AAE when reading an SAE passage, and observations of this phenomenon are not unusual. Approximately half of this third grader's variations from print reflected the operation of an AAE feature.

For reading, features tend to be primarily phonological, or combinations of phonological and morpho-syntactic types. Morpho-syntactic features are infrequent (Thompson et al., 2004). The sample in Table 9.1 is

TABLE 9.1
Example of an Oral Reading Passage From the GORT–3
by a Third-Grade African American Girl (Variations from print
are underlined and features of AAE are numbered.
Substitutions and additions are indicated on the line below)

---

1. Harriet Tubman lived most of <u>her</u> life working to free her people. As a
          all

2. young slave, she ran away to the North. But frequently she returned to the

3. <u>South</u>[1] to help other <u>slaves</u>[2] <u>escape</u>[3]. She became a famous leader of the
   /saʊf/   slave   /ɛkskep/

4. Underground Railroad, a secret network of households that <u>provided</u>[4] food and
                                                            provide

5. shelter to runaway slaves. Harriet led groups of slaves from one point to

6. another <u>on</u> the <u>perilous</u> journey north. They <u>traveled</u>[5] only after nightfall,
          one   /pɜˈlɛriəs/   travel

7. hiding during the day in basements, fields, and forests. <u>Harriet</u> was a master of
                                                            Harriet Harriet

8. tricks and disguises, and at one time a reward of <u>$40,000</u> was offered
                                                    40,000

9. <u>for her capture</u>. Her daring rescues helped hundreds of slaves escape to
   to capture her

10. freedom. As she once said, "I never lost a passenger."

---

1 = /f/ for /θ/
2 = Zero Plural/Consonant Cluster Reduction
3 = Consonant Cluster Movement
4 = Zero Past
5 = Zero Past/Consonant Cluster Reduction

From "Gray Oral Reading Tests–Third Edition," by J. L. Wiederholt and B. Bryant, 1992. Copyright 1992 by Pro-Ed. Adapted with permission.

consistent with this pattern. Fortunately, methods are available that avoid penalizing African American students for being dialect speakers when reading a test passage aloud. For example, scoring modifications are available to credit the Accuracy Score on the GORT when variations from print are consistent with AAE features (Craig, Thompson, Washington, & Potter, 2004; Harber, 1982). Scoring adjustments are important because they make it less likely that AAE variations will be misinterpreted as evidence of a reading disability.

The early findings were consistent in showing no relationship between production of morpho-syntactic and/or phonological features and reading performances (Gemake, 1981; Goodman & Buck, 1973; Harber, 1977; Hart, Guthrie, & Winfield, 1980; Melmed, 1973; Rystrom, 1973–1974; Seymour & Ralabate, 1985; Simons & Johnson, 1973; Steffensen et al., 1982). The consensus in this literature overall was that dialect was not related to reading outcomes for African American students and, accordingly, this line of research was not pursued. Only a few scholars have continued to discuss a potential relationship between AAE and academic achievement (Adler, 1992; Manning & Baruth, 2000).

Bartel and Axelrod's (1973) study of ninth-grade African American students who were reading at either a fourth-grade or an eighth-grade level was a rare exception to the findings noted above. They found a significant difference in the frequencies with which students in the two groups produced selected dialect features. Unfortunately, they did not report levels of dialect produced by the two groups, or the direction of the difference. The tenor of the discussion, however, suggested that the lower group, comprised of students reading at the fourth-grade level, produced more dialect forms than the group reading at the eighth-grade level on a sentence repetition task and during oral reading of sentences from the GORT.

We have suggested elsewhere that some AAE speakers seem to make a tradeoff between achieving SAE accuracy and rate (Craig et al., 2004). There is no way to know how many times the student in Table 9.1 silently switched to an SAE form prior to speaking. The many potential decision points, however, likely slowed her down. As can be seen in Table 9.1, "slaves" was read (line 3) with the plural -s omitted, consistent with the *zero plural* feature of AAE, but plural -s was included when "slaves" was read in lines 5 and 9. Similarly, the *consonant cluster movement* feature was evident in her pronunciation of "escape" in line 3, but not in the same word in line 9, and so on. Fluency resulting from the combined processes of accuracy and rate may be hampered when AAE speakers try to read in SAE (Craig et al., 2004). Our proposal is consistent with earlier work by Harber (1982) who found that African American students read more slowly than their mainstream peers on an earlier version of the GORT (Form C, Gray & Robinson, 1967). The recently published GORT–4 (Wiederholt & Bryant, 2001) provides a longer time to read stories, which may be of particular value to AAE-speaking students on this test.

The research heuristic in the early studies involved selecting a small set of features known to characterize adult AAE and then probing for links to reading scores. Dependence upon a few selected adult AAE features represented a serious limitation in this work. With the development of a more comprehensive inventory for child AAE, and of the DDM as a metric for characterizing dialect density, now we are better situated to probe for potential AAE–reading linkages.

Dialect Shifting and Reading

Students who speak AAE demonstrate a gradual shift in dialect use toward SAE, which is evident around 7 to 8 years of age (Bountress, 1983; Fishman, 1991; Isaacs, 1996; Wolfram, Adger, & Christian, 1999). As discussed in chapter 5, we also observed a significant downward shift in dialect production rates, measured using the DDM, between kindergarten and first grade (Craig & Washington, 2004a). Morpho-syntactic features characterized discourse during picture descriptions, and the shift at first grade substantially reduced production of the morpho-syntactic features (Craig & Washington, 2004a). These data provide empirical support to prior proposals that African American students learn to dialect shift as part of their formal schooling (Adler, 1992; Battle, 1996; Fishman, 1991).

Dialect shifters outperformed nonshifters on measures of reading achievement (Craig & Washington, 2004a). Reading achievement was assessed by the schools, and the instruments included: the total reading score from the Iowa Tests of Basic Skills (Hoover, Dunbar, & Frisbie, 2001); the reading score from the TerraNova (1997); the total reading score from the Metropolitan Achievement Tests (1993); and the mean of the Story and Informational subtests of reading from the Michigan Educational Assessment Program (1999–2001), which is the State of Michigan's required test of school achievement. Similarly, Charity, Scarborough, and Griffin (2004) found that greater "familiarity" with SAE, as measured by exact repetition of SAE sentences during an elicited imitation task, was associated with better reading scores on the Woodcock Reading Mastery Tests–Revised (WRMT–R, Woodcock, 1987) by second- through fifth-grade African American students. In addition, Connor (2002) found that racially Black students who spoke SAE scored well above the mean on a set of measures predicting decoding skills, whereas preschoolers in the Black racial group who spoke AAE scored well below the mean. Together these studies are suggestive of an advantageous relationship between knowledge of SAE and reading acquisition.

In other work, we observed a second shift, at third grade, during oral reading (Craig, Thompson, et al., 2003). Phonological features predominated during reading (Craig, Thompson, et al., 2003; Thompson et al., 2004). Morpho-syntactic features were low frequency in reading, and showed no change from second through fifth grades. Considering these two shifts together, therefore, the shift at Grade 1 substantially reduced production of morpho-syntactic features, and the second shift at Grade 3 substantially reduced production of phonological features (Craig, Thompson, et al., 2003; Craig & Washington, 2004a). We have proposed (Craig, Thompson, et al., 2003) that the timing of the dialect shift for reading, between second and third grades, corresponds to the typical change in reading instruction occurring around the same time, from decoding to comprehension of text (Adams, 1990). Decoding emphasizes phoneme–grapheme relationships, which may facilitate the reduction of phonological features when reading SAE text.

Overall, we understand very little about when and why a child shifts to SAE, or what variables and influences support its acquisition. It is the case that many children seem to learn SAE from the time of daily exposure to it within schools, and strong linguistic skills may play a role. However, if SAE has limited currency in one's daily life, for example, if it is not needed to interact with Mom and Dad, play with siblings, negotiate with a peer, buy a treat from the local store, then why learn it? Assimilation likely requires active integration of SAE forms with daily functions. Passive observation of SAE, as when a child watches television, will not support the kinds of integration required to become a competent speaker of SAE. Even programs on television that have educational goals tend to emphasize concepts and vocabulary rather than the contrastive morpho-syntax and phonology distinguishing AAE and SAE. If the child is motivated to read, text may provide the opportunity for active integration of SAE in a context that has increasing meaning to the child. A beneficial reciprocal relationship between decoding and dialect shifting may emerge for some students, so that dialect shifting improves the correspondence between phonemes and graphemes and decoding highlights the forms, which vary between AAE and SAE.

In summary, linguistic skill bears a marked positive relationship to reading achievement for African American students. Students with better language skills acquire dialect-shifting abilities as part of early schooling. Furthermore, better readers demonstrate greater sensitivity to SAE. Two periods of dialect shifting during oral production occur across the elementary grades. Morpho-syntactic features decrease as part of a shift downwards in dialect feature production rates at first grade for oracy tasks. Phonological features decrease as part of a second shift at third grade for reading. Considered together, these recent studies indicate that increased awareness and use of SAE are associated with better reading outcomes for African American students.

Reading Tests

It is not possible to advance understanding of the reading achievement of African American students unless valid assessment instruments are available. Our research program primarily has been examining the Gray Oral Reading Tests (GORT–3, Wiederholt & Bryant, 1992; GORT–4, Wiederholt & Bryant, 2001). It is widely used, standardized, and yields subtest as well as global performance scores.

We have found that performances of African American students on the GORT–3 evidence no gender or SES bias, and scores distribute normally with appropriate statistical spread (Craig et al., 2004). Performances on the GORT–3 also show strong associations to performances on other reading tests: the Iowa Test of Basic Skills (ITBS, Hoover et al., 2001), Metropolitan Achievement Test (MAT, 1993), and the Michigan Educational Assessment Program (MEAP, 1999–2001). These characteristics recommend the GORT for use with African American students.

The various editions of the GORT depend to a large extent upon the student's oral reading of passages of increasing length and complexity. Reading aloud can be informative for African American students because it provides the examiner with an opportunity to observe AAE production during reading. Most variations on the GORT that are attributable to the use of AAE involve the phonological feature system (Craig, Thompson, et al., 2003; Harber, 1982; Thompson et al., 2004). There is no reason to believe that if a student produces AAE features while reading aloud, that the features are not also present during silent reading. Whereas many tests are timed, students learning to dialect shift read more slowly and thus may be disadvantaged at particular times throughout the process of acquiring SAE.

Scoring corrections have been developed for the GORT (Craig et al., 2004; Harber, 1982) so that students' accuracy scores do not treat as errors any variations from print that are consistent with features of AAE. It is important for practitioners to use these scoring adjustments with African American students. We found (Craig et al., 2004) that the overall performance scores (Oral Reading Quotient [ORQ]) increased significantly when they were applied to the performances of a group of African American second through fifth graders. We recommend that the reader adopt the AAE scoring adjustments when administering and scoring the GORT with African American students. It is not always apparent at the time of test administration for what purposes a score may ultimately be used. The higher AAE–ORQ score would be more valid in any cross-student comparison, for example, between minority and mainstream students in a class or school. It is important to remember that these are *performance* scores, not statements about a student's *ability* to improve his or her reading skills.

The statistical difference that we found had only limited educational impact (Craig et al., 2004). A measurable difference of two Standard Score points between unadjusted (SAE–ORQ) and adjusted (AAE–ORQ) overall scores were observed, increasing the average scores from 90.4 to 92.5. This small change impacted only 3% of the participant sample. Specifically, on the SAE–ORQ, 30% of the students fell more than one standard deviation (< 85) below the performance mean (100), and on the AAE–ORQ, 27% of the students fell more than one standard deviation below the mean. Nevertheless, for interpretive purposes, the adjusted AAE–ORQ is more appropriate.

There is no evidence that AAE relates to Comprehension scores on the GORT (Craig et al., 2004; Harber, 1982). The Comprehension subtest presents a series of multiple-choice questions after each passage. Whereas AAE manifests itself primarily as a set of morpho-syntactic and phonological features, these feature systems operate at the level of the word or phrase. Accordingly, successful selection of the targeted multiple-choice response may relate less to word and phrases and more to the student's understanding of meanings represented by larger linguistic units like the sentence, or discerning the gist of the paragraph.

Overall, considerable information is accumulating about the usefulness of the GORT for African American students. This test appears to be appropriate when examiners want to determine how an African American student will perform reading SAE texts. It would be helpful if future research examined other widely used reading assessment instruments to determine their appropriateness for African American students, so that educators are better able to guard against cultural bias in their reading outcome data.

Syntax, Vocabulary, and Reading Skills

Most research on language–literacy relationships for African American students has focused on AAE–reading linkages, as discussed earlier. Our research program is beginning to examine nondialectal aspects of language, particularly syntax and vocabulary abilities, and their relationships to reading skills.

Syntax is a major aspect of language, and the development of complex syntax is a major early achievement for children (Brown, 1973; Owens, 2001; Tager-Flusberg, 2001). The development of complex syntax is critical to success in the literacy contexts of classrooms (Jackson & Roberts, 2001; Scott, 2004). In particular, teacher directions frequently are multiclausal and thereby incorporate complex sentence structure relationships. Text employs a large number of syntactic structures at a high rate compared to spoken discourse (Bus, 2001). Even books designed for the early grades use complex syntax to develop core concepts for time and place, and interactions between story participants. Syntactic structure provides an interpretive context for children when trying to identify unfamiliar words (Gleitman & Gillette, 1999). As can be seen in the reading passage from the GORT presented in Table 9.1, the ability to formulate and comprehend multiclausal sentences is a component skill for reading. Furthermore, many language disorders are characterized by problems acquiring complex syntax (Leonard, 1998; Paul, 2001; Rice, 2000).

In our research program, we have found that many African American students with language disorders show weak syntactic skills compared to their chronological peers (Craig & Washington, 2000). Further, complex syntax skills at school entry predicted later reading achievement (Craig, Connor, et al., 2003) for African American students from LSES and MSES homes. We estimated that for every 1% rate of increase in complex syntax production at school entry, performances on MAT scaled scores increased by 2.4 points at third grade.

Vocabulary is another important language skill undergirding reading success. Once a student has sounded out the letters in a word, making the appropriate sound–letter correspondences, he or she must recognize the word. Word recognition depends on an adequate vocabulary, and proficient African American readers evidence a greater breadth of vocabulary than struggling readers (Thompson & Craig, 2005). However, vocabulary skill involves more than a large repertoire of recognizable words. Students must learn that the same word may play various roles, for example as a synonym or an antonym, and that its role contributes additional depth of meaning. They must also learn that the same word can be flexible, having multiple meanings in different contexts. African American students who are proficient readers far surpass their peers who are struggling readers in both depth and flexibility of vocabulary knowledge (Thompson & Craig, 2005).

ORAL LANGUAGE AND WRITING

Theoretically, AAE feature production may influence spelling and sentence generation, and writing samples are a potentially revealing context for their study. Scott and Rogers (1996) reviewed and critiqued early studies from the 1970s and noted that most suffered from major methodological flaws. Kligman and Cronnell (1974) was a notable exception. Like studies of the era that searched for AAE–reading linkages discussed in a prior section of this chapter, Kligman and Cronnell selected a relatively small set of specific features. They compared the oral and written spelling of second graders and found dialect-related spelling errors. Compared to White students, African American students made 3 times the number of spelling errors of the White students, and 5 times the number of errors on words that could take a dialect feature. Kligman and Cronnell also observed that oral and written productions of features were not identical. For example, past tense deletions were more likely to occur during writing. DeStefano (1972) also found differences in the distributions of AAE features between writing and speaking for African American fifth graders. Noun features were more likely to occur during writing whereas verb features were more likely to occur during speaking.

By way of illustration, Tables 9.2 and 9.3 present samples of spontaneous story writing by African American students enrolled in our research program. As can be seen in these tables, two thirds of the nonstandard word and sentence forms in Table 9.2 and all in Table 9.3 are consistent with AAE features. The students in the two examples differ considerably from each other. The student in 9.2 is struggling more. She has difficulty with the mechanics of writing, including punctuation and penmanship, and the story lacks coherence. Both students, however, were similar in that they produced a number of AAE features. Thompson, Craig, and Washington (2004) found that more than half (62%) of their third graders produced AAE features in their writing samples. Amounts of feature production varied considerably across students, from no features to a high of one feature for every approximately four written words. Phonological features were infrequent in the writing context. Feature production in the written samples involved morpho-syntactic features and combinations of morpho-syntactic and phonological types. Again, this is illustrated in Tables 9.2 and 9.3, in which the students produced primarily morpho-syntactic or combination features.

The rate of AAE feature production during writing is much lower than in the spoken discourse of picture description (Thompson et al., 2004). It is important to recall that AAE is an oral variation of English and has no conventionalized written equivalent. Students hear spoken AAE but likely do not read it. Whereas many African American students have limited experience with storybooks and other forms of text prior to school entry, first exposure to written text beyond environmental print occurs with entry into formal schooling. These early exposures are in the form of SAE written language. Perhaps dialect shifting is context dependent, and learning SAE may be best supported in writing (Thompson et al., 2004).

Writing is a context where fewer students use dialect, despite continued high levels for speaking (Thompson et al., 2004). The writing of stories seems well suited to strengthen dialect-shifting skills because compared to speaking, writing doesn't require such rapid processing. Furthermore, the self-generation of passages of written text removes the comprehension burden of reading the words of others.

TABLE 9.2
A Writing Sample From a Third-Grade Boy With Good/Average
Cognitive Skills but Weak Vocabulary
(From an MSES Family Residing in Metropolitan Detroit)

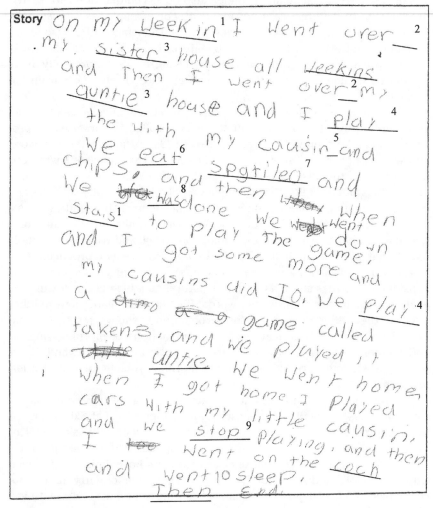

1 = Consonant Cluster Reduction
2 = Zero Preposition
3 = Zero Possessive/Post-vocalic Consonant Reduction
4 = Zero Past/Post-vocalic Consonant Reduction
5 = Zero Plural/Consonant Cluster Reduction
6 = Zero Past
7 = Zero Plural/Post-vocalic Consonant Reduction
8 = Subject–Verb Agreement
9 = Zero Past/Consonant Cluster Reduction

TABLE 9.3
A Writing Sample From a Third-Grade Girl With Good/Average
Language and Cognitive Performance Skills
(From an MSES Family Residing in Metropolitan Detroit)

Story

One day a dog name[1] zipper got a big bone.
He was a very happy dog. One day zipper
had[2] saw a girl name[1] Jazmine. She was
in a big hole. She said, "Zipper,
Zipper, help, help." zipper had[2] got up and
went to get help and when he came
back with the fair[3] men she[4] so happy so
(fire) [4]
when she came out She had[2] gave
zipper a big hug and said, "Thank you."
And that is how zipper became a
hero.

The End

1 = Zero Past/Consonant Cluster Reduction
2 = Preterite Had
3 = Neutralization of Diphthong
4 = Zero Copula

Issues raised in this chapter underscore the importance of having teachers who are familiar with child AAE. Otherwise, they may treat dialectal variations as reading (Cunningham, 1976–1977; Markham, 1984; Piestrup, 1973) or writing errors. Teachers who are not armed with knowledge of AAE may confuse reading and writing errors, and dialectal variations from print, both as evidence of literacy problems and inappropriately place low expectations on the student's performance.

SUMMARY

Once again, Malik exemplified many of the issues raised in this chapter. Malik was one of the African American students in our participant sample who did not spontaneously dialect shift to SAE. Table 1.1 shows that between preschool and fourth grade his rate of feature production actually increased. We suggested in this chapter that the spontaneous shift to SAE forms within school settings occurs for many students in the absence of direct instruction, and this appears associated with stronger linguistic skills overall. In contrast to this pattern, Malik failed to dialect shift and his overall language skills, as discussed in the last chapter, were weak compared to his peers. Malik's fourth-grade teacher characterized his overall classroom performance as below average, and judged that he would likely graduate high school but not continue on to college. The teacher's ratings were more accurate than the parent's or Malik of himself.

In summary, unlike the early research, current studies indicate that AAE is related to reading outcomes, when viewed more expansively as a feature set, rather than in terms of isolated links between specific features and reading scores. Dialect shifting develops spontaneously for significant numbers of elementary-grade African American students and adoption of mainstream linguistic forms is positively associated with reading achievement.

10

SUMMARY AND FINAL THOUGHTS

The year 2004 marked two important legal anniversaries for African American children. It was the 50th anniversary of *Brown v. Board of Education* (1954) and the 25th anniversary of *Martin Luther King Junior Elementary School Children v. Ann Arbor School District Board* (1979). *Brown v. Board of Education* opened all public schools to African American children. The *Ann Arbor* decision attempted to improve the ability of AAE-speaking students to learn to read once they had access to excellent schools. Twenty-five years after the *Brown* decision, the *Ann Arbor* decision was needed to remedy reading failure, and 25 years later, we continue to be concerned about low academic achievement overall and the central place of low reading performances within that problem.

Most African American students in the state of Michigan, like their peers around the country, are not able to pass the state's standardized reading test. They continue to be part of a persistent Black–White Test Score Gap for a broad set of academic achievements. Considerable research has focused on the language of African American students, particularly in speech–language pathology, and has contributed a substantial body of new information in recent years. The National Research Council Report in 1998 (Snow et al., 1998) refocused concern on the lack of reading achievement for minority students and the role of language in these processes.

The goal of this book has been to summarize and situate the work of our research program at the University of Michigan in this important line of inquiry. In order to summarize this information, this final chapter relates the major findings back to Malik, and then concludes with suggestions for future research.

MALIK GOES TO SCHOOL (AND FAILS)

Malik entered public schooling at Preschool. He was an engaging young child who was cooperative and responsive, seeming to enjoy the tasks and activities that we presented him. His language skills at preschool were comparable to his peers in most areas. However, his receptive syntax skill, measured by performance on the RevS tasks, was not at grade level. In addition, Malik spoke AAE, and as a preschooler his DDMs were lower than his peers.

Like a large proportion of African American students, Malik lived in an LSES home in a large urban setting. The literature indicates that students like Malik are high risk for academic failure. Often home literacy levels are low and books and other written materials may not be available to the young student. Unlike many African American students around the country, however, Malik attended schools in a district with high-quality government-funded preschool programs, with overall financial resources that were as good as or better than most school districts in the state. Malik's family valued education and had high hopes for Malik's future. Despite these hopes and resources, Malik's outcomes were poor.

Unfortunately, Malik failed at school. At second grade he was having difficulty with reading and writing, and his achievement levels declined as he proceeded through the elementary grades. By fourth grade his reading achievement was poor, and other academic subjects were suffering as well. Like many low-income African American students entering school, Malik's language skills were average, but not impaired. However, his heritage language skills were weak: His DDM was low for his grade. We have proposed that language skills are a buffer, and by implication, inattention by schools to development of strong language skills may ensure the academic failure of students like Malik. Based on our recent research, it is not surprising that Malik failed to achieve basic reading levels. His general oral language skills were adequate at preschool but his dialect levels revealed lack of facility with the language of the community. This lack of dialect skill suggests that he would not adapt linguistically to the language of the classroom. His fourth-grade DDMs confirmed that this was the case. When his peers were reducing the amount of AAE in classroom contexts, Malik was increasing it. Based on what we now know about relationships between dialect-shifting skill and reading outcomes, his low DDMs at preschool were a risk factor. In retrospect, Malik likely would have benefited from a program of prevention focused on enriching and strengthening all language skills.

CUMULATIVE RISK AND RESILIENCY MODEL

We have suggested elsewhere (Craig & Washington, 2004b) that no single variable can account for the difficulties experienced by students like Malik. Our approaches must address the interdependent and complex relationships involved in being an AAE speaker, living in an AAE-speaking community, and educated in a different linguistic system. Most risk factors for African American students center on poverty and its co-variables, especially differences in literacy experiences prior to schooling. There is no doubt that poverty and its co-variables present a formidable barrier to learning. Unfortunately, much of the research with African American children is from low-income homes and has isolated only a few variables for study, rather than considering combinations of explanations and their interactions (Vernon-Feagans, Hammer, Miccio, & Manlove, 2001). Vernon-Feagans and colleagues suggest that understanding of low achievement would be improved by adopting a "cumulative risk model." Our own work suggests that this proposal is an important one, and offers an important conceptual framework for future research. The research indicates that a host of variables likely impact achievement outcomes. These include: poverty and associated low family literacy levels, higher health risks, poorer quality classrooms and teachers. These also likely include low teacher expectations, and a gap between family and school perceptions and expectations. Student perceptions are also part of the problem, often reflecting unrealistic assessments of their performance and minimal effort at working toward high achievement.

Our own research program indicates that oral language skills are an important and often neglected factor in predicting achievement outcomes, but that they are only one factor. Recalling the proposals of Rutter (1987) and Sameroff, Seifer, Barocas, Zax, and Greenspan (1987), a child faced with only one barrier to literacy acquisition may not be at risk for reading difficulties, whereas a child facing multiple barriers may be. Accordingly, an African American child entering school who is an AAE speaker but has weak language skills, and also is from an LSES home with limited exposure to literacy materials of any type, has a parent with low literacy levels, and is faced with a teacher who has low expectations, is high risk for reading failure compared to the child who faces only one of these barriers. Conceivably, these risk factors load against him or her, and may converge in different ways at different developmental stages and for various educational tasks.

The Black–White Test Score Gap crystallizes the problems with achievement of African American students and has shown little improvement to date. The Black–White Test Score Gap remains large, is widespread, and is not simply explained by the disproportionately high levels of poverty among African American families. Future research needs to continue to identify risk factors, and to consider the intersections among these variables at critical times in the learning process.

It will be important for future research not to focus only on risk factors, but to identify resiliency factors as well. What variables play a positive role in academic success? A thought-provoking aspect of the extant literature on African American students and the Black–White Test Score Gap is the observation that some students beat the odds. For example in Detroit, 30% don't fail (Standard & Poor's School Evaluation Services). We need to understand these children. It would be constructive to devote as much scholarly effort to understanding resiliency factors and success as we currently do on risk factors and failure. For example, research published in 2004 (Charity et al., 2004; Craig & Washington, 2004a) indicates that strong linguistic skills may counter some of the negative influences faced by African American students. Most African American students residing in large urban centers speak AAE and it appears that those with stronger linguistic skills adapt to the SAE of the classroom and curriculum by shifting toward SAE in speaking and reading. Are there other factors like oral language, which can be used within general education frameworks to improve outcomes?

Oral language is clearly a child-centered skill that is shaped by the environment and life experiences. Are there other important internal influences that have not been considered fully? For example, temperament, motivation, drive, personality, and sense of identity all seem like good candidates for co-variates. How do these child variables interact positively or negatively with the environment? If known, relative responses by educators that maximize the child's unique strengths may offer new ways to strengthen the child's paths for learning.

The substantial amounts of research conducted over the past decade have improved tremendously our understanding of the language of African American elementary-grade students. How can practitioners use this information, and how can students like Malik benefit? We are now in a position to identify African American students with language disorders. Most critically, we are also able to characterize African American students like Malik who demonstrate weak language developmental skills. This represents important gains in our ability as educators to identify children who need language intervention, and children who would benefit from strong prevention programs that may improve later attempts at teaching these children to read. Well-funded early language and literacy programs hold great promise for improving outcomes for significant numbers of African American students. As part of the No Child Left Behind Act (2002), the Early Reading First and Reading First initiatives represent notable examples of ways in which schools can infuse classrooms with language, and thereby improve the reading performance of young children. These initiatives provide educators with general education models for developing the linguistic foundations for later reading and for reading across the content areas.

The promise of these early prevention programs provide a glimmer of hope for young children entering our nation's preschools and for those enrolled in early elementary grades. These children represent the future of reading—a future that is hopeful for improved reading ability in high-risk populations. However, the outlook currently is not as hopeful for children like Malik who are older, and have not had the benefit of participating in these new initiatives. They are the students who will enter middle and high school with significant deficits in reading production and comprehension. The intersection between language and literacy development suggests that strengthening early language skills is critical, but in the absence of attention to these early skills, how will we as a nation ensure the development of older, able readers? What intervention models are appropriate for a child who is 11, 12, 14, 16 years old who has not attained desirable reading levels? Will it be important to focus on language skill development with these older poor readers, as it would be with their younger counterparts? Alternatively, does the focus for these older children rest with strengthening weak, print-specific literacy skills, with little need for attention focused on their oracy skills?

In conclusion, despite tremendous amounts of new information about African American students, far too many questions remain unanswered. It is our hope that this book will provide practicing clinicians and beginning teachers with a framework for interpreting the new research that will continue to emerge. In addition, we hope that the case of Malik and the many students like him, will provoke discussion and future research. Given what we have learned over the last decade, we now would have approached Malik differently. It is our hope that in another 10 years, we will be even better equipped to recognize his risk status early on, and to implement appropriate preventative measures.

Once students arrive at the school room door, they become the responsibility of the school and all the professionals and administrators involved in educating the child. It is imperative that general education-based solutions become available. Let's not wait until the only solution for students like Malik is intervention on a special education caseload.

LIST OF APPENDIXES

Appendix A: Methods and Examples of Transcripts and Coding Systems, as discussed in chapter 3

Appendix B: Additional Comments and Examples of AAE Features, as discussed in chapter 4

Appendix C: Feature Production Rates Relative to Race of Examiner, SES, and Gender, as discussed in chapter 5

Appendix D: Additional Discussion and Scoring Details for the Expressive and Receptive Language Measures, as discussed in chapter 6

Appendix E: Complex Syntax Scoring Taxonomy, as discussed in chapter 6

Appendix F: Optional Prompts for the Wh-question Task

Appendix G: African American Family Survey: Caregiver Questionnaire

Appendix H: AAE Features Checklist, as discussed in chapter 7

APPENDIX A

This appendix provides more description of the methods used to transcribe, segment, score, and analyze the language sample data discussed in chapter 3.

Transcription

C-units were transcribed into CHAT (Codes for the Human Analysis of Transcripts) files using the conventions of the Child Language Data Exchange System (CHILDES, MacWhinney, 1994). The advantages to using one of the currently available computer software programs for transcription purposes are many. Our transcription process required a number of passes through the transcribed text. These included: (1) creation of a draft transcript from the audiotape or other medium, (2) creation of a final draft transcript, (3) creation of a separate transcript for reliability analyses by another individual, and then transfer of the file to an individual for scoring. For our research program, a primary advantage of computerized transcripts was shared file use with established conventions across transcripts and transcribers. Table A.1 presents a portion of a transcript using CHAT conventions and our codes.

Segmentation

The core decision in using C-unit segments relates to determining where the boundaries are within multi-unit sequences of discourse. For our language samples, this required segmenting successive main clauses linked by simple coordinate conjunctions into separate C-units if the second clause included statement of a subject. When the second clause omitted the subject through ellipsis, the two clauses were scored as a single C-unit. For example, (1) below was segmented into two C-units (indicated by the /) because the subject in the clause following the coordinate conjunction was stated, and (2) below was scored as a single C-unit because the second clause elliptically omitted the subject.

(1) *she made um like a circle/ and then <u>she made something</u>*

(2) *um the peoples fall down and <u>go on the snow</u>*

Using Loban's criteria, elliptical responses that were not full clauses were considered single C-units if they were responses to prior adult questions. For example, in the transcript presented in Table 3.3, when the examiner asked: *frenchfries and what?* The student responded elliptically: *hamburger and frenchfries*, and the student's response was considered a single C-unit. Similarly, we scored as single C-units stereotypical acknowledgments (*yes, no, oh, okay, mmhm*, etc.) when they were responses to either prior adult questions or comments, and *what?* when produced by the student as a clarification request.

We have examined mean length of C-unit (Loban, 1976) production within our research program in order to contribute to the development of a

A Portion of Malik's Transcript Presented in Table 3.4 With
the CHAT Conventions Indicated and the AAE and Csyn Codes

```
@Begin
@Participants:      CHI child, ADU XXX
@ID:                XXX
@Sex of XXX:        male
@Birth of XXX:      XX-XXX-XXXX
@Age of XXX:        4;8.0
@Date:              XX-XXX-XXXX
@Location:          XXX School
@Situation:         Picture Description
@Transcriber:       XXX
@Phonology:         XXX
@Coder:             XXX


@bg:    Accident
*ADU:   ok tell me about this picture.
*CHI:   it-'is emergency.
%AAE:   $ZAR
*ADU:   mmhm.
*CHI:   and the bike.
*ADU:   mmhm.
*CHI:   broke.
*CHI:   jacket.
*CHI:   car.
*CHI:   man.
*CHI:   lady.
*ADU:   ok.
*ADU:   what-'is go-ing on in the picture?
*CHI:   somebody got dead off the bike.
%SYN:   $GER
*CHI:   and they hit something.
*CHI:   this hit the car.
*ADU:   what else?
*CHI:   and this put <the>[/] the jacket-s.
*ADU:   ok.
*CHI:   he had fell.
%AAE:   $HAD
*CHI:   and the car run-ed over him.
*ADU:   ok is that all?
*CHI:   and him was go play basketball.
%AAE:   $UPC $ING $ZTO
%SYN:   $ISS
*ADU:   ok lets try the next one.
@eg:    Accident
```

Note. Reformulations are indicated by < >. AAE was the coding file name assigned to the morpho-syntactic features. Mor coding tiers preexisted in CHAT and thus was unavailable as a coding file for our purposes. XXX substitutes for participant identifying information in the tables to preserve confidentiality. AAE morpho-syntactic codes: $ZAR = Zero article; $HAD = Preterite *had*; $UPC = Undifferentiated pronoun case; $ING = Zero -*ing*; $ZTO = Zero *to*. Syntax codes: $GER = Gerunds and participles; $ISS = Simple infinitive with same subject.

quantified set of oral language expectations for typically developing African American students. C-units were selected because they were appropriate across the full span of grades we have been studying. Words were selected instead of morphemes as the base in these calculations because so many of the AAE features operate at the level of the morpheme compared to the word (see examples of the features in chapter 4) and the rules for their inclusion or exclusion are not fully understood. Adopting the word-based count thus allowed us to calculate changes in formulation-unit lengths relatively independently from the morpho-syntactic variations.

Scoring

In order to develop the complex syntax scoring taxonomy, transcripts were examined for all C-units that were formulated with more than one main verb, expressed either explicitly or elliptically (Craig & Washington, 1994). The types of complex syntax that these represented were then identified using Bloom and Lahey (1978), Brown (1973), Miller (1981), Fletcher and Garman (1988), and Owens (1988) as resources. More than one instance of AAE features or types of complex syntax was possible within a single C-unit. In the following example, the C-unit was scored for multiple instances of AAE features and complex syntax.

He[1] waitin'[2] until[3] she say[4] go[5].
[1]Zero copula [2]G-dropping [3]Conjunction [4]Subject–verb agreement [5]Noun phrase complement

Coding files for AAE features and for complex syntax were created within CHILDES and analyzed with CLAN (Computerized Language Analysis). The CLAN program automatically tallied the frequencies of AAE and of complex syntax using the frequency command (FREQ). Average C-unit lengths in words were calculated using the mean length of turn command (MLT). In addition, word lists were generated using the FREQ command that were adapted for analysis of numbers of different word types within language samples. See chapter 6 for discussion of these measures. Tables A.2 to A.5 present sample outputs from CLAN. Table A.2 shows that the student produced a total of 33 instances (tokens) of 8 different AAE features (types). Table A.3 shows that the student produced a total of 19 instances (tokens) of complex syntax. Of this total, six different types of complex syntax were produced. Table A.4 displays MLT, the ratio of words over C-units, the raw values for computing MLT (i.e., ratio of words over utterances = 6.59), and the number of turns represented in the student's language sample. For our transcripts, utterances are C-units. Table A.5 shows that the student produced a total of 45 words (tokens) and 29 different words (types). This in-

CLAN Output From FREQ Command for AAE Codes

Tokens and types of AAE codes

```
> freq XXXpd3.cha +t%AAE -t*
FREQ XXXpd3.cha +t%AAE -t*
FREQ is conducting analyses on:
 ONLY dependent tiers matching: %AAE;
*****************************************
From file <XXXpd3.cha>
20 $cop
 1 $dmk
 2 $eit
 2 $fsb
 1 $neg
 4 $sva
 1 $upc
 2 $zto
----------------------
    8 Total number of different word types used
   33 Total number of words (tokens)
0.242 Type/Token ratio
```

Note. AAE morpho-syntactic codes: $COP = Zero copula; $DMK = Double marking; $EIT = Existential *it*; $FSB = Fitna/Sposeta/Bouta; $NEG = Multiple negation; $SVA = Subject–verb agreement; $UPC = Undifferentiated pronoun case; $ZTO = Zero *to*.

TABLE A.3
CLAN Output From FREQ Command for SYN Codes

Tokens and types of complex syntax (csyn) codes

```
> freq XXXpd3.cha +t%SYN -t*
FREQ XXXpd3.cha +t%SYN -t*
FREQ is conducting analyses on:
 ONLY dependent tiers matching: %SYN;
*****************************************
From file <XXXpd3.cha>
 9 $con
 5 $ger
 1 $ids
 1 $inc
 2 $iss
 1 $uni
----------------------
    6 Total number of different word types used
   19 Total number of words (tokens)
0.316 Type/Token ratio
```

Note. Syntax codes: $CON = Clauses joined by conjunctions; $GER = Gerunds and participles; $IDS = Infinitive with a different subject; $INC = Incompletes; $ISS = Simple infinitive with same subject; $UNI = Unmarked infinitive.

TABLE A.4
CLAN Output From MLT Command

Mean length of c-unit

```
> mlt XXXpd3.cha
MLT XXXpd3.cha
MLT is conducting analyses on:
 ALL speaker tiers
*****************************************
From file <XXXpd3.cha>
MLT for Speaker: *CHI:
 MLT (xxx and yyy are INCLUDED in the utterance and morpheme
counts):
    Number of: utterances = 22, turns = 6, words = 145
      Ratio of words over turns = 24.167
      Ratio of utterances over turns = 3.667
      Ratio of words over utterances = 6.591

MLT for Speaker: *ADU:
 MLT (xxx and yyy are INCLUDED in the utterance and morpheme
counts):
    Number of: utterances = 9, turns = 7, words = 45
      Ratio of words over turns = 6.429
      Ratio of utterances over turns = 1.286
      Ratio of words over utterances = 5.000
```

cludes the hand editing completed for this transcript. Words that had the same root word but different inflections (e.g., sidewalks) were counted as a single instance (token) of the same word type. Abbreviations that represented distinct words (e.g., that's and that is) were added separately.

Reliability Measures and Statistical Approaches

The portions of the samples used for reliability studies were determined randomly and then transcribed a second time by an independent examiner. Percentage agreements were then calculated by summing the number of agreements between the original and reliability transcripts, and by dividing this number by the combined number of agreements plus disagreements. For transcription reliabilities, point-to-point comparisons were made at the level of the morpheme because the targeted child AAE features in most of our work were morpho-syntactic in nature. As the phonological feature system has been developed, each transcript is listened to again in its entirety by an independent transcriber for phonological features. Point-to-point comparisons have been made at the level of the feature. Scoring agreements were 85% or higher across all analyses.

A word list for the number of different words (NDW) analysis

```
> freq XXXpd3.cha
FREQ XXXpd3.cha
FREQ is conducting analyses on:
  ALL speaker tiers
*****************************************
From file <XXXpd3.cha>
  5 a
  2 all
  1 ambulance
  6 and
  1 bike
  1 book-s
  2 broke-en
  2 bush-s
  2 car
  2 fall-ing
  1 fire
  1 hand-s
  1 hold-ing
  1 lunch+box
  1 paper
  2 people
  1 share-ing
  1 sidewalk
  1 sidewalk-s
  1 sign
  1 sled-ing
  1 slide-ing
  1 snowman
  1 soccer
  1 soccer+ball
  1 stop+sign
  2 that-'is  +1
  1 tree-s
  1 yell-ing
----------------------
   29  Total number of different word types used −1 +1 =  29
   45  Total number of words (tokens)
0.644  Type/Token ratio
```

Interpretation of the data was facilitated using a number of different statistics. Statistically significant differences were determined using Multiple Analysis of Variance Models (MANOVA), post hoc Tukey Honestly Significant Differences (HSD) to probe for the source of the differences observed, and Bonferroni Correction where alpha levels were adjusted for potential relatedness within the data sets by dividing the experiment-wide p value of .05 by the number of measures. For example, if four language measures were found to be highly correlated and derived from the same language samples, the p value was divided by this number of measures and a more conservative significance level adopted ($.05/4 = .0125$).

As our measures became more refined and research designs expanded to ask more complicated questions, Hierarchical Linear Modeling techniques were applied to the data (HLM, Bryk, Raudenbush, & Congdon, 1996). HLM allowed for analysis of changes in behaviors over time, the attainment of targeted levels of behaviors, and the variables influencing these measures of growth.

APPENDIX B

This appendix provides the definitions of the morpho-syntactic, phonological, and combination features of child AAE, along with examples. For some features, additional scoring comments are provided.

Morpho-Syntactic Features of Child AAE

Ain't. *Ain't* used as a negative auxiliary in *are+not*, *is+not*, *have+not*, and *do+not* constructions. Although adults use *ain't* as part of a tag question (Washington & Craig, 2002), children don't. The students in our research program do produce tags although not frequently, and not using *ain't*.

Example of *ain't* in an are+not construction.
Child: *and the cars <u>ain't</u> gonna move.*

Example of a tag question without *ain't*.
Child: *yeah you're gonna carry your own, <u>aren't</u> you?*

Appositive pronoun. A pronoun is used in addition to a noun, or a second pronoun, to signify the same referent.

Example of a noun and appositive pronoun.
Child: *<u>the crossing guard she</u> whistling to him to make the car stop and um so the boy can get her his papers.*

Example of a pronoun and appositive pronoun.

Child: *and then* <u>*this one*</u> <u>*he*</u>*'s down on the ground with a carpet.*

As children get older, the phrase modifier may expand to a clause modifier. The two elements are not necessarily adjacent but may include modification of the first element between the first element and the pronoun, as in the following examples.

Example of a phrase modifying the noun prior to the appositive pronoun.

Child: <u>*the man with the red shirt*</u> *he he* <u>*he*</u> *covered his eye 'cause he didn't wanna see it.*

Example of a clause modifying the noun prior to the appositive pronoun.

Child: <u>*this man*</u> <u>*that ran over him*</u> <u>*he*</u>*'s &um got a bandage on his head because maybe his head's hurt.*

Completive *done*. *Done* and *did* used to emphasize a recently completed action.

Example of completive *done*.

Child: *he* <u>*done*</u> *fall down.*

Example of completive *did*.

Child: *and they &fe and they* <u>*did*</u> *fell.*

Double marking. Multiple agreement markers are used for irregular plural nouns, pronouns (especially possessive pronoun <u>mines</u>), and hypercorrection of irregular verbs. For children, these double mark number or verb tense.

Example of double marking an irregular plural noun for number.

Child: *then the* <u>*peoples*</u> *in the car is smashed.*

Example of double marking a pronoun for number.

Child: *what's* <u>*thems*</u> *doing?*

Example of double marking an irregular verb for past tense.

Child: *a boy* <u>*was*</u> *hur<u>ted</u> on the floor.*

Example of double marking an irregular verb for number.

Child: *they* <u>*fells*</u>.

Double copula/auxiliary/modal. Two modal auxiliary forms, used in a single clause, is a feature of adult AAE. For children, two copula or auxiliary forms of the verb *to be* may be produced. In our research program, we have not elicited double modals until the middle elementary grades. For example, a fourth-grade girl said: "*she said she might try to find a private school that he might can go to.*" Examples of forms produced by preschoolers and kindergartners follow.

Example of double copula.
Child: *I'm is the boy.*

Example of double auxiliary.
Child: *they're is playing in snow.*

Existential *it*. *It* is produced in place of *there* to indicate the existence of a referent without adding meaning. Picture description is a high frequency context for eliciting this form from children.

Example of existential *it*.
Child: *and a shovel not sposeta be in there 'cause it's no snow.*

Fitna/sposeta/bouta. The words *fixing to*, *supposed to*, and *about to* are produced as abbreviated forms coding imminent action.

Example of *fitna* coding imminent action.
Child: *he fitna slide.*

Example of *sposeta* coding imminent action.
Child: *this thing sposeta go on it.*

Example of *bouta* coding imminent action.
Child: *he bouta slip on the in the street.*

Preterite *had*. *Had* is added before simple past verbs.

Example of preterite *had*.
Child: *then that little girl had fell in.*

Indefinite article. *A* is used regardless of whether the onset of the subsequent noun is a vowel.

Example of *a* substituting for *an*.
Child: *&umm a boy is giving his friend &um <u>a</u> airplane.*

Invariant *be*. Infinitival *be* is used to express habitual or extended actions and states.

Example of invariant *be* coding an extended action.
Child: *they <u>be</u> learning how to skate.*

Multiple negation. Two or more negatives are used to express negation. The mixing of positive and negative terms is avoided so that all potential forms for expressing negation are consistently marked.

Example of negative auxiliary and pronoun in combination.
Child: *but <u>nobody</u> <u>doesn't</u> make a eight.*

For AAE, multiple negatives reinforce negation. This contrasts, for example, to "*and nobody doesn't like Sara Lee!*" which is an affirmation.
Regularized reflexive pronoun. *Hisself, theyself, theirselves* replace regular forms of the reflexive pronouns *himself, themselves.*

Example of *hisself* substituting for *himself.*
Child: *then the other boy hurt <u>hisself</u> on the head.*

Example of *theyself* substituting for *themselves.*
Child: *everybody stop and hurt <u>theyself</u>.*

Example of *theirselves* substituting for *themselves.*
Child: *and the people on the other side they skating there all by <u>theirself</u>.*

Remote past *been*. *Been* coding action in the remote past is an AAE feature, but was rarely ever produced by preschoolers or kindergartners in our program of research over the last 10 years.

Example of remote past *been*.
Child: *I <u>been</u> know that.*

Subject–verb agreement variations. Subjects and verbs are produced with differences in marking of number. These include omission of the 3rd person singular number marker *-s* on main verbs, and differences in the relationships between subjects and auxiliaries.

Example of omission of the 3rd person singular marker on a main verb, in the /s/ form.

Child: *and then the school, the the kids are waiting 'til he pick_ stuff up.*

Example of omission of the 3rd person singular marker on a main verb, in the /z/ form.

Child: *I don't know who it belong_ to.*

Example of omission of the 3rd person singular marker on a main verb, in the /ɪz/ form.

Child: *so now that teach_ you not to mess with Batman.*

Example of differences in number between the singular subject and plural auxiliary form of *to be*.

Child: *everybody are getting hurt.*

Example of differences in number between the plural subject and singular auxiliary form of *to be*.

Child: *but the other girl and boy and boy was laughing.*

Example of differences in number between the subject and modal auxiliaries *do* and *have*.

Child: *he don't wanna move.*

Child: *and his wheel have busted open.*

Undifferentiated pronoun case. Pronoun cases are used interchangeably. Objective and nominative cases substitute for each other.

Example of an objective case substituting for a nominative case pronoun.

Child: *me don't know.*

Example of the reverse, in which a nominative case substitutes for an objective case pronoun.

Child: *that car ran he over.*

Example of an objective case substituting for a demonstrative pronoun.

Child: *and that boy dropped all them paper.*

Objective case pronouns substituted for possessive pronouns, which we considered to be an example of the Zero possessive feature discussed below.

Example of an objective substituting for a possessive case pronoun.

Child: *and him lose him papers on the floor.*

Zero article. Articles are variably included and excluded.

Example of omission of *a*.
Child: *I'll set them up in _ minute soon as I get this somewhere.*

Example of omission of *an*.
Child: *police officers and _ ambulance was there.*

Example of omission of *the*.
Child: *can you push it into _ bottom for me?*

Zero copula. *Is, are, am* and other forms of the verb *to be* are variably included or excluded in either copula or auxiliary form.

Example of omission of copula *to be*.
Child: *because he _ cold.*

Example of omission of auxiliary *to be*.
Child: *this one _ not feeling better.*

Zero -ing. Present progressive *-ing* is variably included or excluded.

Example of omission of *-ing*.
Child: *and here's a lady that's that's wear_ pink.*

Zero modal auxiliary. *Will, can, do*, and *have* are variably included or excluded as modal auxiliaries.

Example of omission of *will*.
Child: *when _ my dad get here?*

Example of omission of *can*.
Child: *maybe we _ take this off.*

Example of omission of *do*.
Child: *_ you have a bowl?*

Example of omission of *has* and *have*.
Child: *I'm gonna change her clothes 'cause she _ been baseballing.*
Child: *I_ never seen it.*

Zero past tense. The *-ed* marker for simple past is variably included and excluded on regular past verbs. Many may also be considered phonological combination features because cluster reduction is involved (see the next section). Present forms of irregulars are used as well.

Example of omission of the *-ed* marker.
Child: *and he almost slip_.*

Example of producing the present form of an irregular past verb.
Child: *that man had picked that little boy up and <u>take</u> him to a doctor.*

Zero plural. The plural *-s* marker on nouns is variably included and excluded, and includes /s/, /z/, and /ɪz/ phonological forms.

Example of omission of the plural *-s* marker, in the /s/ form.
Child: *wait ten minute_.*

Example of omission of the plural *-s* marker, in the /z/ form.
Child: *I see him dropping his paper_ in the street running to get 'dem.*

Example of omission of the plural *-es* marker, in the /ɪz/ form.
Child: *and some kids got their lunchbox_ and books and stuff in their hands.*

Zero possessive. Possession is coded by word order so the possessive *-s* marker is omitted, and includes /s/ and /z/ phonological forms. We also code **zero possessive** when the case of the possessive pronoun is changed, although this might be considered another example of **undifferentiated pronoun case**.

Example of omission of the possessive *-s* marker, in the /s/ form.
Child: *a student papers fell.*

Example of omission of the possessive *-s* marker, in the /z/ form.
Child: *somebody_ bike broke.*

Example of using a pronoun other than in the possessive case.
Child: *they was playing with <u>they</u> skate.*

Zero preposition. Prepositions are variably omitted.

Example of omission of the preposition *to.*
Child: *what happened _ the tree?*

Example of omission of the preposition *at.*
Child: *I play _ home.*

Example of omission of the preposition *by*.
Child: *he &um he got runned over __ a car.*

Example of omission of the preposition *of*.
Child: *and the boy fell out __ the car.*

Example of omission of the preposition *in/into*.
Child: *and the boy he got __ a accident.*

Example of omission of the preposition *for*.
Child: *she's supposed to make dinner __ the Barbie.*

Zero to. Infinitival *to* is variably included and excluded.

Example of omission of the infinitive *to*.
Child: *he was trying __ run after them.*

Phonological Features of Child AAE

The phonological features used by first through fifth graders within our research program are the following. Phonological features are written phonemically in / / under the word that was changed, and phonemic substitutions are further indicated in brackets (/).

Consonant cluster movement. The reversal of phonemes within a cluster. This may involve consonant reduplication, or may be a change in order without reduplication.

Example of consonant cluster movement with reduplication.
Child: *her daring rescues helped hundreds of slaves escape to*
                                                            /ɛkskep/
    freedom.

Example of consonant cluster movement without reduplication.
Child: *I ask my mom or something.*
    /æks/

Devoicing final consonants. Voiceless consonants substitute for voiced following the vowel.

Example of devoicing final consonant.
Child: *and a lady told the man to stop and they're sad.*
              /tolt/ (t/d)   /sæt/ (t/d)

Postvocalic consonant reduction. Consonant singles are omitted following vowels.

Example of postvocalic consonant reduction.
Child: *and the car broke.*
/bro/

"g" dropping. Substitutions of /n/ for /ŋ/.

Example of "g" dropping.
Child: *and this boy is getting ready to fall.*
/gɛtʔɪn/

Substitutions for /θ/ and /ð/. /t/ and /d/ substitute for /θ/ and /ð/ in prevocalic positions and /f, t/ and /v/ substitute for /θ/ and /ð/ in intervocalic and postvocalic positions.

Example of /d/ substituting for /ð/ preceding the vowel.
Child: *somebody dropped their paper.*
/dɛɚ/ (d/ð)

Example of /t/ substituting for /θ/ between vowels.
Child: *or probably the boy had to just walk low without letting the*
/wɪtaʊt/ (t/θ)
crossing guard know.

Example of /v/ substituting for /ð/ between vowels.
Child: *and let the other cars so they won't crash into the papers.*
/ʌvɚ/ (v/ð)

Example of /f/ substituting for /θ/ after the vowel.
Child: *and everybody had they mouth open.*
/maʊf/ (f/θ)

Example of /t/ substituting for /θ/ after the vowel.
Child: *that's the little boy that's sitting down with a cover over.*
/wɪt/ (t/θ)

Consonant cluster reduction. Deletion of phonemes that are part of a consonant cluster.

Example of consonant cluster reduction.
Child: *oh all right first there was a car crash.*
/fɚs/

Syllable deletion. Omission of an unstressed syllable in a multisyllabic word.

Example of syllable deletion.
Child: *and then all of a sudden he fell because she let <u>because</u> he*
                                                          /kʌz/
          let go.

Syllable addition. Addition of a syllable to a word, usually as a hyper-correction.

Example of syllable addition.
Child: *and the driver on the purple in the purple car is <u>stopped</u>*   ·
                                                          /stɑptɪd/
          'cause the guard put her stop sign up for they won't run over the boy
          paper.

Monophthongization of diphthongs. Neutralization of diphthongs.

Example of monophthongization of diphthongs.
Child: *it is a lady blowin' a whistle at a stop <u>sign.</u>*
                                                  /sɑn/ (ɑ/aɪ)

Combinations of Morpho-syntactic and Phonological Features

Five of the morpho-syntactic features could combine with two of the phono-logical features and these were designated as 7 combinations. Labov, Baker, Bullock, Ross, and Brown (1998) argue that *past tense consonant cluster reduction* is a phonological rather than morpho-syntactic rule. However, this proposal has not yet been confirmed and awaits additional research for children. Accordingly, we simply designated these as combinations, and these are listed below with examples.

Example of consonant cluster reduction + zero past tense.
Child: *and he <u>slip</u> and fell.*

Example of consonant cluster reduction + zero plural.
Child: *and the two kids are holding their <u>book</u> and going walking home to-*
          gether.

Example of consonant cluster reduction + subject–verb agreement.
Child: *a little kid is showing the &uh other little kid a &um what a what a tri-*
          angle <u>look</u> like.

Example of postvocalic consonant reduction + zero past.
Child: *and then they try to save 'em.*

Example of postvocalic consonant reduction + zero plural.
Child: *and he on his knee sort of bending down.*

Example of postvocalic consonant reduction + zero possessive.
Child: *somebody bike got broken.*

Example of postvocalic consonant reduction + subject–verb agreement.
Child: *because she probably like know_ him or care_ about him.*

APPENDIX C

This appendix provides supplementary information for the distributional relationships presented in chapter 5.

Race of Examiner

Table C.1 summarizes statistically nonsignificant findings across studies for potential race of examiner effects. Whether an examiner was Black or White was not significantly related to student outcomes across a number of measures and comparisons.

TABLE C.1
Statistical Comparisons of Language Outcomes
for African American and White Examiners

Measure	Statistic	Source
PPVT–III Standard Scores	$t(57) = .641, p > .05$	Washington & Craig, 1999
Likelihood of passing or failing screening assessment	$t(194) = -1.31, p = .193$	Washington & Craig, 2004
DDMs Picture Description for first to fifth graders	$t(293) = 1.2, p = .24$	Craig & Washington, 2004a
DDMs Picture Description for third graders	$t(48) = 1.6, p = .11$	Thompson et al., 2004
DDMs Reading for third graders	$t(48) = 1.2, p = .22$	Thompson et al., 2004
DDMs Writing for third graders	$t(48) = 0.36, p = .72$	Thompson et al., 2004

Note. DDM = dialect density measure.

The studies summarized above were between-student comparisons and do not directly answer the question of whether race of examiner exerts systematic influences on the dialect produced by students. It would have been better to obtain repeated measures on the same child with different examiners, rather than grouped-comparisons data as represented above.

We have looked directly at the race of examiner issue for responses to the Wh-questions task, which we developed as an assessment instrument. Like responding to the PPVT–III (Washington & Craig, 1999), the race of examiner exerted no systematic effect. Unlike the studies summarized in Table C1, however, we compared repeated measures with the same student but two different examiners. One examiner was African American and spoke AAE and the other examiner was White and spoke SAE. The performances of 40 kindergartners, approximately one third from the mid-size central city and two thirds from the urban-fringe community, showed no statistically significant differences between examiners,[1] for these within-student comparisons.

What these analyses tell us is that groups of young children on average use dialect at equivalent levels regardless of the dialect production level of the adults. Any change from typical language production likely requires some level of metalinguistic skill. The student must be able at some level to reflect on his or her own dialect production and alter it based on the partner. Many of the students in our research program were probably too young to have developed metalinguistic skills of this type. The relationships between metalinguistic skill and dialect shifting are potentially interesting, but await future investigation.

SES and Gender

Both SES and gender were related to the amounts of feature production occurring in the children's discourse. LSES kindergartners produced more features during free play than MSES peers, and boys produced more features during free play than girls. See Table C.2.

TABLE C.2
Production of AAE Features for Kindergartners,
Calculated as Tokens/50 C-Units

	LSES		MSES		Combined	
	M	SD	M	SD	M	SD
Males	13.1	4.6	9.4	3.8	11.0*	4.5
Females	10.9	5.2	6.6	4.1	9.1	5.2
Combined	11.8**	5.0	8.0	4.1		

Note. From "Socioeconomic status and gender influences on children's dialectal variations," by J. A. Washington and H. K. Craig, 1998, *Journal of Speech, Language, and Hearing Research, 41*, p. 622. Copyright 1998 by the American Speech-Language-Hearing Association. Adapted with permission.
*$p < .05$. **$p = .001$.

---

[1]$t(39) = 1.18$; $p = .25$.

No statistically significant relationships were found between the DDMs during picture description and either SES or gender for 400 preschool through fifth graders. See Table C.3.

TABLE C.3
Production of AAE Features for Preschoolers Through
Fifth Graders, Calculated as DDMs: Tokens/Words

	LSES		MSES		Combined	
	M	SD	M	SD	M	SD
Males	.071	.057	.051	.045	.058	.050
Females	.061	.052	.048	.043	.053	.047
Combined	.065	.054	.050	.044		

Note. Based on data reported in Craig and Washington, 2004a.

A number of methodological differences were apparent between these studies. Although both studies used morpho-syntactic features as the basis for the calculations, the kinds of measurements differed, as well as the elicitation context. However, it is unlikely that the measurement differences were responsible for the differences between studies. Whereas the Washington and Craig report allowed the number of words to vary within the 50 C-unit samples, and the Craig and Washington report controlled for differences in the numbers of words, it is possible that the control at the word level rather than the C-unit level removed the SES and gender differences observed in the first report. This seems unlikely, however, as Washington and Craig reported statistically nonsignificant differences in MLCU. In fact, the utterances were longer with an MLCU mean of 3.52, standard deviation = .53 for the LSES kindergartners, compared to 3.23, standard deviation = .49 for the MSES kindergartners. Similarly, when analyzed by gender, the MLCUs for the boys and girls were not different statistically.

APPENDIX D

This appendix provides additional information about the measures described in chapter 6 for characterizing selected nondialectal characteristics of the oral language skills of typically developing African American students. Tables D.1, D.2, D.3, and D.4 report outcomes for four measures of expressive language, and the three receptive language measures, that the reader may find useful as a set of performance expectations for typically developing African American students in preschool through fifth grade.

EXPRESSIVE LANGUAGE SKILLS

TABLE D.1
Means (*M*) and Standard Deviations (*SD*)
for Measures Calculated From Picture Descriptions

Grade		C-units	MLCU	Csyn	NDW
Preschool	M	22.1	4.38	.24	2.41
n = 66	SD	8.3	1.22	.18	.63
Grades			(P–5)	(P–5)	(P–5)
Kindergarten	M	19.6	5.08	.40	2.77
n = 39	SD	6.3	1.46	.28	.79
Grades		(3–5)	(P, 3–5)	(P, 2–5)	(3–5)
1	M	23.4	6.02	.45	3.02
n = 39	SD	6.9	1.15	.24	.61
Grades			(P, 3–5)	(P, 3–5)	(P, 4–5)
2	M	24.2	6.41	.52	3.18
n = 60	SD	8.0	1.43	.25	.72
Grades			(P–K, 4–5)	(P–K, 4–5)	(P, 5)
3	M	27.2	6.99	.64	3.37
n = 69	SD	10.9	1.50	.28	.74
Grades		(K)	(P–1, 5)	(P–1, 5)	(P–K, 5)
4	M	27.8	7.33	.69	3.55
n = 63	SD	11.4	1.39	.28	.77
Grades		(K)	(P–2)	(P–2)	(P–1)
5	M	26.9	7.85	.82	3.78
n = 64	SD	9.6	1.92	.32	.84
Grades		(K)	(P–3)	(P–3)	(P–3)

Note. The first- through fifth-grade data are from "Oral Language Expectations for African American Children in Grades 1 Through 5," by H. K. Craig, J. A. Washington, and C. A. Thompson, in press. Significant grade relationships (Grades) are identified in parentheses.

Numbers of C-units Produced During Picture Description

Statistically significant grade differences characterize the number of C-units produced while describing a constant set of three pictures.[2] Preschoolers showed no consistent grade-related patterns, but the kindergartners did. The kindergartners were not significantly different from the preschoolers, or the first or second graders. They were significantly less productive than the third through fifth graders. The first through fifth graders were not significantly different from each other.

---

[2]$F(6, 399) = 4.42, p = .000.$

MLCU

As can be seen from the data reported in Table D.1, statistically significant grade differences characterize C-unit production lengths.[3] As Craig, Washington, et al. (2004) observed, MLCUs were not statistically different from the immediately preceding or following grade. MLCUs increased significantly, however, when more than one grade span was examined. For example, the MLCUs of the first graders were significantly longer than those of the preschoolers. They were significantly shorter than those produced by third graders. However, they were not statistically different from those of the kindergartners or second graders.

Gender differences were apparent on this measure.[4] The MLCUs of the girls were slightly greater ($M = 6.5$, $SD = 1.8$) than the boys ($M = 6.2$, $SD = 1.9$).

Complex Syntax

Table D1 reports the proportional frequencies for Csyn, calculated as the number of Csyn tokens in a language sample collected during picture description relative to the number of C-units in the sample. Appendix E presents the scoring system for complex syntax. Statistically significant grade differences were apparent,[5] and these differences were between nonconsecutive rather than consecutive grades. Performances varied systematically on this measure relative to gender.[6] The Csyn for the girls were slightly greater ($M = .58$, $SD = .32$) than the boys ($M = .50$, $SD = .33$). Performances on Csyn did not vary by SES.

NDWs

Word lists formed the basis for the NDW analyses and were generated automatically using the FREQ command of CLAN. FREQ generated complete word lists from the target sample and then we edited these lists so that morphological variations in the form of number and tense markers on regular nouns and verbs were ignored. A noun like *girl* was counted as a single lexical type regardless of whether it was spoken as *girl* or *girls*. A verb like *walk* was counted as a single type regardless of whether the sentence context required it to be formulated as *walk*, *walks*, *walking*, or *walked*. As a result, only the number of different lexical roots was represented in these

---

[3] $F(6, 399) = 42.7$, $p = .000$.
[4] $F(1, 399) = 6.54$, $p = .011$.
[5] $F(6, 399) = 40.2$, $p = .000$.
[6] $F(1, 399) = 11.14$, $p = .001$.

analyses, and variations due to dialectal differences were not part of this calculation.

Like MLCU and Csyn, NDW varied significantly by grade,[7] and again these differences were between nonconsecutive grades. Like MLCU and Csyn, NDW varied significantly by grade,[8] and again these differences were between nonconsecutive grades. See Table D.1.

RECEPTIVE LANGUAGE SKILLS

Receptive Vocabulary

Table D.2 summarizes the mean PPVT–III standard scores for preschoolers (Washington & Craig, 1999) and for another new 235 students (72 LSES, 163 MSES), enrolled in Grades 1 to 5. Preschoolers whose primary caregiver had attained high school graduation or better scored significantly better than the preschoolers whose caregiver had not matriculated from high school. Similarly, first through fifth graders who were children of college graduates performed significantly better on this test than students whose caregivers had less education.

TABLE D.2
Mean (*M*) PPVT–III Standard Scores and Standard Deviations (*SD*)
for African American Students Relative to the Educational
Level of Their Primary Caregivers

Caregiver Education	Preschoolers[1] (n = 55)		Grades 1–5 (n = 235)	
	M	*SD*	*M*	*SD*
College graduate	94.0	12.3	103.2[2]	13.3
High school graduate	93.2	8.8	95.9	12.9
Less than high school	77.3	10.7	93.0	13.0

Note. The data for preschoolers are from "Performances of At-Risk, African American Preschoolers on the Peabody Picture Vocabulary Test–III" by J. A. Washington and H. K. Craig, 1999, *Language, Speech, and Hearing Services in Schools, 30*, p. 79. Copyright 1999 by the American Speech-Language-Hearing Association. Adapted with permission.
[1]$F(2, 50) = 4.35; p < .05$.
[2]$F(2, 232) = 8.10; p = .000$.

-----

[7]$F(6, 399) = 26.1, p = .000$.
[8]$F(6, 399) = 26.1, p = .000$.

Responses to Wh-Questions (Wh-q)

Table D.3 presents the response values on the Wh-q task for 400 typically developing African American preschool through fifth graders. Grade was a systematic source of variation for responses on the Wh-question task.[9] The preschoolers produced significantly fewer correct responses than all of the other grades. The kindergartners and first graders each produced significantly more correct responses than the grades below them, and significantly fewer correct responses than the grades above them. The second through fifth graders also produced significantly more correct responses than the preschoolers through first graders. Another grade difference was

TABLE D.3
Means (*M*) and Standard Deviations (*SD*)
for Responses on the Wh-Questions Task (Wh-q)

	Wh-q	
Grade	*M*	*SD*
Possible Points = 72		
Preschool	49.3	7.9
n = 66		
Grades	(K–5)	
Kindergarten	54.1	7.7
n = 39		
Grades	(P, 1–5)	
Possible Points = 114		
1	100.3	6.2
n = 39		
Grades	(P–K, 2–5)	
2	104.3	5.0
n = 60		
Grades	(P–1, 5)	
3	106.0	4.7
n = 68		
Grades	(P–1)	
4	107.2	4.5
n = 63		
Grades	(P–1)	
5	108.3	3.7
n = 64		
Grades	(P–2)	

Note. The first- through fifth-grade data are from "Oral Language Expectations for African American Children in Grades 1 Through 5," by H. K. Craig, J. A. Washington, and C. A. Thompson, in press. Significant grade relationships (Grades) are identified in parentheses.

---

[9]$F(6, 399) = 1188.8$, $p = .000$.

observed between Grades 2 and 5, but not the grades in between these. In other words, although correct responding continued to increase after second grade, the span of grades necessary to detect significant increases in performance was quite large.

Responses to Reversible Sentence Probes of the Active/Passive Voice Distinction (RevS)

Prompts on this task were comprised of one active voice prompt and two passives. When developing the task, as expected, young children evidenced confusion when responding to the passive trials. Occasionally, the demands of these passive trials resulted in young students discontinuing the task prior to completion. In order to facilitate responding and maintain the interest and cooperation of even preschoolers, we constructed the final version of the task to present two active voice trials but only one passive voice trial.

All of the prompts and pictures shared the following additional characteristics: (1) all agents and actions readily lent themselves to the picture format; (2) all agents and actions were familiar to the children and could be identified easily by them during pretesting; (3) all pictures were in the form of simple black line drawings and presented on 5 × 7 inch cards; (4) 10 common nouns and verbs were selected that avoid potential asymmetries in response probabilities relative to the likelihood of the reversibility of the actions occurring in real-life experiences; and (5) the passives and the simple present tense active verbs limited the influence of strong AAE feature contrasts on the task. The 10 sets of picture pairs were randomly ordered. The three spoken trials that accompanied each picture pair were randomized as well. This high level of randomization within the RevS task was necessary because pilot testing indicated that there was a statistically significant order effect on nonrandomized trials. There was an advantage if the child was presented with both active trials prior to the passive trial (Craig et al., 1998b).

The scoring of the RevS task had two components. First, at the time of administration, the examiner noted on-line whether the child's picture point was a match to the spoken prompt using a simple plus/minus notation system. Second, after administration of the task, responses were evaluated for comprehension of the active and passive voice by assigning one point for comprehension of the active voice and one point for comprehension of the passive voice. Each picture pair received the point score of one for active voice comprehension if both of the active trials were correctly matched to the spoken prompt. Each picture pair received the point score of one for passive voice comprehension if the student pointed to the correct picture in response to the spoken passive prompt, and only if both active trials were responded to correctly for that picture as well. Recalling that the student was presented with two active voice trials but only one passive voice trial to maximize the response levels of the youngest students, the scoring represented a conservative approach to evaluation of the passive trials. Scoring of the passive maintained a balance between the active and passive voice trials in the total score on the task, and avoided weighting the total scores toward the correct active voice trials. Total possible points was 20.

RevS showed a steadily increasing performance score with grade from preschool through second grade. Statistically, the grade effects were significant.[10] Preschoolers had fewer correct responses than any of the other grades. Kindergartners had more correct responses than preschoolers, but fewer than the other grades, and first graders had more correct responses than either the preschoolers or kindergartners, but fewer correct responses than the second through fifth graders. The second through fifth graders were not different from each other. As reported by Craig, Washington, et al. (2004), after second grade, the values remained essentially the same, around 18.5 points. We noted that the standard deviations steadily decreased across grades. These two findings were suggestive of a ceiling effect at second grade, where the response values did not change beyond second grade and the performances of groups of students showed less and less variation around this average response value.

Table D.4 presents the preschool through second-grade scores out of a possible total RevS score of 20. By the end of second grade, most typically

TABLE D.4
Means (*M*) and Standard Deviations (*SD*) for Responses on the RevS

	RevS	
Grade	*M*	*SD*
Preschool	12.0	3.9
n = 49		
Grades	(K–5)	
Kindergarten	15.0	3.7
n = 24		
Grades	(P, 1–5)	
1	17.7	2.5
n = 18		
Grades	(P–K)	
2–5	18.4	2.0
n = 22		
Grades	(P–K)	

Note. The first- through fifth-grade data are from "Oral Language Expectations for African American Children in Grades 1 Through 5," by H. K. Craig, J. A. Washington, and C. A. Thompson, in press. Significant grade relationships (Grades) are identified in parentheses.

[10]$F(6, 399) = 45.6, p = .000.$

developing African American students comprehend the active/passive voice distinction in sentences.

APPENDIX E

This appendix provides a scoring taxonomy for the complex syntax features as discussed in chapter 6.

Simple infinitive with same subject (ISS)

> Utterances containing verb infinitives in which the subject is the same for both the main verb and the infinitive. Those involving early catenatives were not included, for example: *gotta, gonna, wanna, hafta, sposeta*, and *fitna*, for example: "me and her *fitna* leave this on."

> <u>Examples</u>
> "and somebody's trying **to pull** him back up"
> "and a boy stopped in the middle of the street **to get** his papers"

Simple noninfinitive *wh*-clause (NIW)

> The *wh*-clause is followed by a subject plus verb, rather than an infinitive.

> <u>Examples</u>
> "he's showing him **what he made**"
> "I don't know **what they're called**"

Noun phrase complement (NPC)

> Utterances in which a full subject and predicate clause replaces the noun phrase, usually in the object position of the main clause. *That* may be included or excluded and the main verbs are usually transitive.

> <u>Examples</u>
> "it looks like **she laughing** at him"
> "and I think **he's sad**"

Let(s)/Lemme and Infinitive (LET)

Utterances in which let, let's, or lemme introduce the main clause.

Examples
"**lemme** cook it"
"okay **let's** see"

Relative clause (REL)

Utterances in which a noun or pronoun in the main clause is modified by another clause. These did not include phrases modified by prepositional phrases, for example: "the boy *in the swimming pool* is standing up."

Examples
"I know something **that can fit** in her hand"
"I think she mad at somebody **who ran over** a car"

Infinitive with a different subject (IDS)

Utterances containing verb infinitives in which the subject of the infinitive is different from the subject of the verb in the main clause.

Examples
"she telling him **to go**"
"then they was waiting for him **to come** out the hospital"

Unmarked infinitive (UNI)

Utterances containing infinitive verbs with the *to* omitted in which the main verb lexically was *let, help, make,* or *watch.* Deletions of *to* judged to be optional omissions and one of the AAE forms were not scored as unmarked infinitives, for example: "he goin' shoppin' (*to*) buy some cameras." Instead, these were scored for the clause structure that would have been assigned if the *to* had been said.

Examples
"and somebody make the cars **(to) stop**"
"they're helping him **(to) get** better"

Wh-infinitive clause (WHI)

Two clauses linked by a *wh*-pronoun such as *what, when, where,* or *how,* in which an infinitive verb follows the *wh*-form.

Examples

"and this person need to tell the little boy **when to stop** because cars be coming"

"these two know **how to skate real good**"

Gerunds and Participles (GER)

Utterances containing nouns formed from verbs + *ing*, or adjectives formed from verbs and ending in *ed, t, en*, etc., respectively.

Examples

"and the car is **messed** up"

"the car lights are **broken**"

Tag questions (TAG)

Clauses added to the end of the main clause that are all positive or that contrast positive and negative relationships between clauses. These do not include single word tags, such as *okay* or *please*.

Examples

"this goes to the Barbie, **doesn't it**?"

"I tricked you, **didn't I**?"

Clauses joined by conjunctions (CON)

The combining of clauses using the listed coordinate and subordinate conjunctions to link co-referential nouns in subject or object sentence roles. These did not include phrase or word coordinations, for example: "it's dogs, cat, *and* another dog" or "me *and* my Granny do"; nor pragmative connectives serving as a form to link two turns and appearing in a sentence initial position, for example, "Yeah *but* don't stick me" in response to an adult question. They did include any clauses with an appropriate subject deletion in one clause when the subject was the same in both clauses, for example: "They sit down *and* watch people."

Examples

and: "and the policeman is blowing a whistle **and** stopping people from going"

but: "and there's people hurting themselves **but** trying not to"

so: "and the crossing guard is blowing his whistle **so** everybody could stop"

if: "my mom's gotta help me ice skate **if** I'm gonna"

because: "people laughed at the little boy **because** he dropped his papers"

since: "it been a long time **since** I saw it"

before: "and these two are helping each other **before** they fall"

until: "he waiting **until** she say go"

while: "I see people lifting up their feet **while** they're skating"

like: "some are skiing **like** they don't know how to ski"

Incompletes (INC)

Attempts at any of the above forms that included omission of clause coordinating conjunctions when ellipsis was not appropriate, or other major sentence elements necessary to determining the type of complex syntax.

Examples

"people are skating **(and)** sledding"

"a car is all broke**(n)** and stuff"

From "The complex syntax skills of poor, urban, African American preschoolers at school entry," by H. K. Craig and J. A. Washington, 1994, *Language, Speech, and Hearing Services in Schools, 25*, pp. 184–185. Copyright 1994 by the American Speech-Language-Hearing Association. Adapted with permission.

APPENDIX F

This appendix provides a listing of prompts by grade that may be considered optional when administering the Wh-q task as presented in chapter 7. We recommend that the clinician consider the prompts listed in Table F.1 as optional in order to shorten the administration time for the Wh-q task when used as part of the MPAL Screening Phase. For example, if the student is a first grader, omit the four prompts listed in the table for first grade.

Note that this potentially reduces the administration by four prompts at first grade, five at second grade, six at third grade and again at fourth grade, and then by seven at fifth grade. If, however, the student has difficulty with the task, it is further recommended that the clinician go back and administer these optional items to be sure that one can accurately assume that the student would respond correctly to these prompts.

TABLE F.1
Wh-q Prompts That May Be Considered Optional at Each Grade

Grade 1	Grade 2	Grade 3	Grade 4	Grade 5
What	What	What	What	What
Whose	Whose	Whose	Whose	Whose
How many	How many	How many	How many	How many
If, what do	If, what do	If, what do	If, what do	If, what do
	What doing	What doing	What doing	What doing
		Which one	Which one	Which one
				Why want?

Note. From "Wh-Question Task," by H. K. Craig and J. A. Washington, 2001. Copyright 2001 by The Regents of the University of Michigan.

African American Family Survey: Caregiver Questionnaire

Name of Child:_____Date of Birth:_____

Name of primary caregiver:_____

Date of Birth:_____

How long has the child lived with you?_____

How many people live in the household?_____

Caregiver Marital status:
    ❏ Single (never married)   ❏ In a relationship

    ❏ Married   ❏ Divorced/Widowed

Spouse/partner's name_____

Spouse/partner's age_____ Relationship to child? _____

How many children do you have?_____

Number of children in the home?_____

Names and ages of children living in the home:

_____

_____

What language other than English is spoken in the home?_____

How far did you go in school?_____

How far did your spouse/partner go in school?_____

What is <u>your occupation</u>? (If retired, please describe former occupation)

(Please describe what you do on your job):_____

_____

What is the occupation of <u>your spouse/partner</u>? (If retired, please describe former occupation _____

(Please describe job):_____

_____

_____

DEVELOPMENTAL/MEDICAL HISTORY:

When you (or child's mother) were pregnant with (child's name _____)
Did you (or child's mother) receive prenatal care?

    ❑ Yes   ❑ No   ❑ I don't know

Were there any problems with the pregnancy?

    ❑ Yes   ❑ No   ❑ I don't know

    If **YES**, please explain:_____

    _____

    _____

Was child born premature?
    ❑ Yes   ❑ No   ❑ I don't know

If **YES**, please indicate how many months premature_____

During pregnancy, did you (or child's mother)
    ❑ drink   ❑ smoke   ❑ experience an injury?

While you (or child's mother) were pregnant did you (she) ever have to stay in the hospital overnight?
    ❑ Yes   ❑ No   ❑ I don't know

    What was the reason for staying in the hospital?_____

At what age did child start to

    crawl? _____   **walk?**_____   **talk?**_____

    Were there any problems with the way s/he

        crawled?_____

        walked?_____

        talked?_____

Did child ever have to stay in the hospital overnight?
    ❑ Yes   ❑ No   ❑ I don't know
    If **YES**, when? _____

    How long did child stay in hospital? _____

    What was the reason for staying in the hospital? _____

Did/does child ever have earaches or ear infections?

    ❑ Yes   ❑ No   ❑ I don't know

    How many times has s/he had an ear infection? _____

    In general, how were the earaches or ear infections treated?_____

Has child's hearing ever been tested?

    ❑ Yes   ❑ No   ❑ I don't know

    If **YES**, <u>when</u> and what were the <u>results</u>?_____

_____

Did child ever have a head injury? (Ever have an accident where s/he got hit in the head?)

     ❑ Yes   ❑ No   ❑ I don't know

    If **YES**, at what age? _____

    What caused the injury?_____

What kind of treatment did (child) receive after the injury?

    ❑ Didn't get treatment   ❑ Medication from doctor

    ❑ Treated it at home/home remedy   ❑ Surgery

    ❑ Went to the emergency room/doctor   ❑ Other_____

    ❑ Hospital stay

      ❑ # of days _____

Did child ever lose consciousness? (e.g., faint)   ❑ Yes   ❑ No

Did/does child seem to be clumsy or have a lot of accidents? ❑ Yes   ❑ No

Please list any allergies the child has: _____

_____

Please list any illnesses the child has and what, if any, prescription medication is taken for it.

Illness   **Medications**

_____   _____

_____   _____

My child (Please check all those that apply)

    ❑ **is a picky eater (foods or textures)**   ❑ **is a messy eater**

    ❑ **coughs/chokes while eating**   ❑ **drools**

FAMILY EDUCATIONAL HISTORY

Do(did) any members of your family have any of the following: (check all that apply)

			Other members of household				
	You	Spouse/	child				

	partner						
Had trouble with writing?							
Had trouble with spelling?							
Had trouble reading?							
Had trouble following directions?							
Had trouble understanding people?							
Had trouble hearing?							
Had a speech problem?							
Took special education classes?							
Had trouble paying attention?							
Had trouble remembering things?							
Had trouble getting along with other kids in school?							
Had ADD or ADHD?							
Repeated grades (got left back in school)							

CHILD'S EDUCATIONAL HISTORY

At what age did child start pre-school? _____

      ❑ Child did not attend preschool

How many days per week does/did child attend preschool?_____

    Is (or was) the pre-school

        ❑ Mostly academic (teach children letters, numbers, reading, counting etc.)
        ❑ Mostly play
        ❑ Child care/ Day care
        ❑ A combination of the above

Where is your child currently in school?_____

    Teacher_____ **Grade**_____

Does your child have a current IEP? ❑ Yes   ❑ No

Please describe any other services your child receives_____

I am concerned about my child's:

    ___ understanding of language   ___ ability to communicate

    ___ speech   ___ reading

    ___ writing   ___ spelling

    ___ math   ___ social interaction

    ___ academic success   ___ self esteem

    ___ attention   ___ behavior

Are there situations in which your child is successful relative to the areas of concern?   ❑ Yes   ❑ No

If **YES**, please describe: _____

_____

Please describe what your child does well. _____

_____

Please describe your child's interests. _____

_____

Do you read to your child?   o Yes   o No
    If **YES**, how often?
        o Daily
        o 4 to 6 days /week
        o 1 to 3 days /week
        o A few times per month (only occasionally)

Approximate minutes per session? _____

CHILD'S SOCIAL/BEHAVIOR HISTORY

In general, how much time outside of school does your child spend with children other than his/her siblings?

_____times/week   _____ hrs/day

In what types of activities?_____

_____

Does your child make friends   o on his own?   owith help?   o easily?
                                    oseldom?   o not at all?

Does your child play with children who are   oyounger?   oolder?
                                                 osame?   oself?

Has your child ever used repetitive behaviors that seemed odd over a period

of time? (for example, hand flapping)   o yes   o no

please describe_____

_____

CHILD'S ACADEMIC HISTORY

PLEASE RATE CHILD ON EACH OF THE FOLLOWING

Academic Development

How well does your child...	N/A	Below Average			Average		Above Average	
Say the alphabet	0	1	2	3	4	5	6	7
Recognize letters	0	1	2	3	4	5	6	7
Write letters or numbers	0	1	2	3	4	5	6	7
Count	0	1	2	3	4	5	6	7
Remember information	0	1	2	3	4	5	6	7
Follow instructions	0	1	2	3	4	5	6	7

Move from one task to the next	0	1	2	3	4	5	6	7
Complete tasks	0	1	2	3	4	5	6	7
Pay attention	0	1	2	3	4	5	6	7
Learn new tasks	0	1	2	3	4	5	6	7

Do you read to your child?   o **Yes** o **No**

    If **YES**, how often?
- ❑ Daily
- ❑ 4 to 6 days /week
- ❑ 1 to 3 days /week
- ❑ a few times per month (only occasionally)

How old was your child when you started reading to him/her? _____

APPENDIX H

All grades:

_____ Subject–verb agreement   Subjects and verbs differ in marking of number
"she **don't** wanna go down"

_____ Zero copula/auxiliary   Copula and auxiliary forms of the verb *to be* are variably included
"and he __ blowing a whistle"
"that __ the boy"

_____ Zero past tense   -*ed* markers are variably included on regular past verbs and present forms of irregulars are used

"he **drop__** the paper"
"and that lady **say** stop"

After first grade:

_____ G dropping   Substitution of "n" for "ng" in final word position
"and they're **slidin_** down the hill"

REFERENCES

Abati, R. (1997, January 25). To an African, "Ebonics" or Black English sounds foreign. *The Detroit News*.

Adams, M. J. (1990). *Beginning to read: Thinking and learning about print*. Cambridge, MA: MIT Press.

Adelman, C. (1999). *Answers in the toolbox: Academic intensity, attendance patterns, and bachelor's degree attainment*. Washington, DC: U.S. Department of Education.

Adler, S. (1992). *Multicultural communication skills in the classroom*. Boston: Allyn & Bacon.

American Speech-Language-Hearing Association. *Demographic Profile of the ASHA constituents*. Retrieved September 23, 2004, from http://www.asha.org/NR/rdonlyres/E3207463-1E07-402B-BDC2-A835A738EB0C/0/13601_1.pdf

Anderson-Yockel, J., & Haynes, W. (1994). Joint picture-book reading strategies in working-class African American and white mother–toddler dyads. *Journal of Speech, Language, and Hearing Research, 37*, 583–593.

Aram, D., & Nation, J. (1975). Patterns of language behavior in children with developmental language disorders. *Journal of Speech and Hearing Research, 18*, 229–241.

Artiles, A. J., & Zamora-Duran, G. (1997). Disproportionate representation: A contentious and unresolved predicament. In A. J. Artiles & G. Zamora-Duran (Eds.), *Reducing disproportionate representation of culturally diverse students in special and gifted education*. Reston, VA: Council for Exceptional Children.

Bailey, G., Maynor, N., & Cukor-Avila, P. (Eds.). (1991). *The emergence of Black English: Texts and commentary*. Amsterdam: John Benjamins.

Baratz, J. C. (1970). Educational considerations for teaching standard English to Negro children. In R. W. Fasold & R. W. Shuy (Eds.), *Teaching Standard English in the inner-city* (pp. 223–231). Washington, DC: Center for Applied Linguistics.

Barnett, W. S. (1995). Long-term effects of early childhood programs on cognitive and school outcomes. *The Future of Children, 5*, 25–50.

Baron, D. (2000). Ebonics and the politics of English. *World Englishes, 19*, 5–19.

Bartel, N. R., & Axelrod, J. (1973). Nonstandard English usage and reading ability in Black junior high students. *Exceptional Children, 39*, 653–655.

Barton, D. (1994). *Literacy: An introduction to the ecology of written language.* Oxford, UK: Blackwell.

Bates, E., & MacWhinney, B. (1989). Functionalism and the competition model. In B. MacWhinney & E. Bates (Eds.), *The crosslinguistic study of sentence processing* (pp. 3–73). New York: Cambridge University Press.

Battle, D. E. (1993). *Communication disorders in multicultural populations.* Boston: Andover Medical Publishers.

Battle, D. E. (1996). Language learning and use by African American children. *Topics in Language Disorders, 16,* 22–37.

Baugh, J. (1983). A survey of Afro-American English. *Annual Review of Anthropology, 12,* 335–354.

Beilin, H., & Sack, H. (1975). The passive: Linguistic and psychological theory. In H. Beilin (Ed.), *Studies in the cognitive basis of language development* (pp. 6–83). New York: Academic Press.

Berko-Gleason, J. (2001). *The development of language* (5th ed.). Boston: Allyn & Bacon.

Bever, T. (1970). The cognitive base for linguistic structures. In J. Hayes (Ed.), *Cognition and the development of language* (pp. 279–362). New York: Wiley.

Biddle, B. J., & Berliner, D. C. (2002). Small class size and its effects. *Educational Leadership, 59*(5), 12–23.

Blake, I. K. (1984). *Language development in working-class Black children: An examination of form, content, and use.* Unpublished doctoral dissertation, Columbia University, New York.

Bloom, L., & Lahey, M. (1978). *Language development and language disorders.* New York: Wiley.

Bountress, N. G. (1983). Effect of segregated and integrated educational settings upon selected dialectal features. *Perceptual and Motor Skills, 57,* 71–78.

Bowey, J. A. (1986). Syntactic awareness in relation to reading skill and ongoing reading comprehension monitoring. *Journal of Experimental Child Psychology, 41,* 282–299.

Bracken, B. A. (1986). *Bracken concept development program.* San Antonio, TX: Psychological Corporation.

Braswell, J. S., Daane, M. C., & Grigg, W. S. (2003). *The nation's report card: Mathematics highlights 2003* (NCES 2004-451). Washington, DC: U.S. Department of Education, Institute of Education Sciences, National Center for Education Statistics.

Braswell, J. S., Lutkus, A. D., Grigg, W. S., Santapau, S. L., Tay-Lim, B. S.-H., & Johnson, M. S. (2001). *The nation's report card: Mathematics 2000* (NCES 2001-517). Washington, DC: U.S. Department of Education, Office of Educational Research and Improvement, National Center for Education Statistics.

Bridgeforth, C. (1984). *The development of language functions among Black children from working class families.* Paper presented at the pre-session of the 35th Annual Georgetown University Round Table on Language and Linguistics, Georgetown University, Washington, DC.

Brooks-Gunn, J., Duncan, G. J., Klebanov, P. K., & Sealand, N. (1993). Do neighborhoods influence child and adolescent development? *American Journal of Sociology, 99,* 353–395.

Brown v. Board of Education. (1954). 347 U.S. 483.

Brown, R. (1973). *A first language: The early stages.* Cambridge, MA: Harvard University Press.

Brown, R., Cazden, C., & Bellugi, U. (1968). The child's grammar from I to III. In J. P. Hill (Ed.), *Minnesota symposium on child psychology: Vol. 38* (pp. 28–73). Minneapolis: University of Minnesota Press.

Brown, I. S., & Felton, R. H. (1990). Effects of instruction on beginning reading skills in children at risk for reading disability. *Reading and Writing, 2,* 223–241.

Bryant, D. M., Peisner-Feinberg, E. S., & Clifford, R. M. (1993). *Evaluation of public preschool programs in North Carolina: Final report.* Chapel Hill, NC: Frank Porter Graham Child Development Center.

Bryk, A., Raudenbush, S., & Congdon, R. (1996). *HLM hierarchical linear and nonlinear modeling with the HLM/2L and HLM/3L programs.* Chicago: Scientific Software International.

Burchinal, M. R., Roberts, J., Riggins, R., Zeisel, S., Neebe, E., & Bryant, D. (2000). Relating quality of center-based child care to early cognitive and language development longitudinally. *Child Development, 71*, 339–357.

Bus, A. G. (2001). Joint caregiver–child storybook reading: A route to literacy development. In S. B. Neuman & D. K. Dickinson (Eds.), *Handbook of early literacy research* (pp. 179–191). New York: Guilford Press.

Bus, A. G., van IJzendoorn, M. H., & Pelligrini, A. D. (1995). Joint book reading makes for success in learning to read: A meta-analysis on intergenerational transmission of literacy. *Review of Educational Research, 65*, 1–21.

Campbell, T., Dollaghan, C., Needleman, H., & Janosky, J. (1997). Reducing bias in language assessment: Processing-dependent measures. *Journal of Speech, Language, and Hearing Research, 40*, 519–525.

Campbell, F. A., & Ramey, C. T. (1995). Cognitive and school outcomes for high-risk African-American students at middle adolescence. Positive effects of early intervention. *American Educational Research Journal, 32*, 743–772.

Catts, H. W. (1991). Facilitating phonological awareness: Role of speech-language pathologists. *Language, Speech, and Hearing Services in Schools, 22*, 196–203.

Catts, H. W., Fey, M. E., Zhang, X., & Tomblin, J. B. (1999). Language basis of reading and reading disabilities: Evidence from a longitudinal investigation. *Scientific Studies of Reading, 3*, 331–361.

Chall, J. S., Jacobs, V. A., & Baldwin, L. E. (1990). *The reading crisis: Why poor children fall behind*. Cambridge, MA: Harvard University Press.

Chapman, R. (1988). Language acquisition in the child. In N. Lass, L. McReynolds, J. Northern, & D. Yoder (Eds.), *Handbook of speech-language pathology and audiology* (pp. 120–124). Toronto, Ontario, Canada: B. C. Decker.

Chamberlain, C., & Madeiros-Landurand, P. (1991). Practical considerations for the assessment of LEP students with special needs. In E. V. Hamayan & J. S. Damico (Eds.), *Limiting bias in the assessment of bilingual students* (pp. 111–156). Austin, TX: Pro-Ed.

Champion, T. B. (2003). *Understanding storytelling among African American children: A journey from Africa to America*. Mahwah, NJ: Lawrence Erlbaum Associates.

Champion, T. B., Seymour, H., & Camarata, S. (1995). Narrative discourse of African American children. *Journal of Narrative and Life History, 5*, 333–352.

Charity, A. H., Scarborough, H. S., & Griffin, D. M. (2004). Familiarity with "School English" in African-American children and its relation to early reading achievement. *Child Development, 75*, 1340–1356.

Chomsky, N. (1957). *Syntactic structures*. The Hague: Mouton.

Cole, L. (1980). *Developmental analysis of social dialect features in the spontaneous language of preschool Black children*. Unpublished doctoral dissertation, Northwestern University, Evanston.

Cole, P. A., & Taylor, O. L. (1990). Performance of working-class African American children on three tests of articulation. *Language, Speech, and Hearing Services in Schools, 21*, 171–176.

Coles-White, D. (2004). Negative concord in child African American English: Implications for Specific Language Impairment. *Journal of Speech, Language, and Hearing Research, 47*, 212–222.

Coley, R. J. (2002). *An uneven start: Indicators of inequality in school readiness. Policy information report*. Princeton, NJ: Educational Testing Service. (ERIC Document Reproduction Service No. ED466473)

Connor, C. M. (2002). *Preschool children and teachers talking together: The influence of child, family, teacher, and classroom characteristics on children's developing literacy*. Unpublished doctoral dissertation, University of Michigan, Ann Arbor.

Connor, C. M., Son, S. -H., Hindman, A. H., & Morrison, F. J. (2005). *Teacher qualifications, classroom practices, family characteristics, and preschool experience: Complex effects on first graders' vocabulary and early reading outcomes*. Manuscript submitted for publication.

Crago, M., & Paradis, J. (2003). Two of a kind? The importance of commonalities and variation across languages and learners. In Y. Levy & J. Schaeffer (Eds.), *Language competence across populations: Toward a definition of Specific Language Impairment* (pp. 97–110). Mahwah, NJ: Lawrence Erlbaum Associates.

Craig, H. K. (1995). Pragmatic impairments. In P. Fletcher & B. MacWhinney (Eds.), *Handbook of child language* (pp. 623–640). Oxford, UK: Blackwell.

Craig, H. K. (1996). The challenges of conducting language research with African American children. In A. G. Kamhi, K. E. Pollock, & J. L. Harris (Eds.), *Communication development and disorders in African American children: Research, assessment, and intervention* (pp. 1–18). Baltimore: Brookes.

Craig, H. K., Connor, C. M., & Washington, J. A. (2003). Early positive predictors of later reading comprehension for African American students: A preliminary investigation. *Language, Speech, and Hearing Services in Schools, 34,* 31–43.

Craig, H. K., Thompson, C. A., Washington, J. A., & Potter, S. L. (2003). Phonological features of child African American English. *Journal of Speech, Language, and Hearing Research, 46,* 623–635.

Craig, H. K., Thompson, C. A., Washington, J. A., & Potter, S. L. (2004). Performance of elementary grade African American students on the Gray Oral Reading Tests. *Language, Speech, and Hearing Services in Schools, 35,* 141–154.

Craig, H. K., & Washington, J. A. (1994). The complex syntax skills of poor, urban, African American preschoolers at school entry. *Language, Speech, and Hearing Services in Schools, 25,* 181–190.

Craig, H. K., & Washington, J. A. (1995). African American English and linguistic complexity in preschool discourse: A second look. *Language, Speech, and Hearing Services in Schools, 26,* 87–93.

Craig, H. K., & Washington, J. A. (2000). An assessment battery for identifying language impairments in African American children. *Journal of Speech, Language, and Hearing Research, 43,* 366–379.

Craig, H. K., & Washington, J. A. (2002). Oral language expectations for African American preschoolers and kindergartners. *American Journal of Speech-Language Pathology, 11,* 59–70.

Craig, H. K., & Washington, J. A. (2004a). Grade-related changes in the production of African American English. *Journal of Speech, Language, and Hearing Research, 47,* 450–463.

Craig, H. K., & Washington, J. A. (2004b). Language variation and literacy learning. In C. A. Stone, E. R. Silliman, B. J. Ehren, & K. Apel (Eds.), *Handbook of language and literacy: Development and disorders* (pp. 228–247). New York: Guilford Press.

Craig, H. K., & Washington, J. A. (2004c). [Teacher, parent, and student ratings of students' abilities]. Unpublished raw data.

Craig, H. K., Washington, J. A., & Thompson, C. A. (in press). Oral language expectations for African American students in grades 1 through 5. *American Journal of Speech-Language Pathology.*

Craig, H. K., Washington, J. A., & Thompson-Porter, C. (1998a). Average c-unit lengths in the discourse of African American children from low income, urban homes. *Journal of Speech, Language, and Hearing Research, 41,* 433–444.

Craig, H. K., Washington, J. A., & Thompson-Porter, C. (1998b). Performances of young African American children on two comprehension tasks. *Journal of Speech, Language, and Hearing Research, 41,* 445–457.

Cunningham, P. M. (1976–1977). Teachers' correction responses to black-dialect miscues which are non-meaning-changing. *Reading Research Quarterly, 12,* 637–653.

Darling-Hammond, L. (1997). *The right to learn. A blueprint for creating schools that work.* San Francisco: Jossey-Bass.

Darling-Hammond, L., & Youngs, P. (2002). Defining "highly qualified teachers": What does "scientifically-based research" actually tell us? *Educational Researcher, 31*(9), 13–25.

Demont, E., & Gombert, J. E. (1996). Phonological awareness as a predictor of recoding skills and syntactic awareness as a predictor of comprehension skills. *British Journal of Educational Psychology, 66,* 315–332.

DeStefano, J. (1972). Productive language differences in fifth-grade black students' syntactic forms. *Elementary English, 47,* 552–558.

DeTemple, J. M. (2001). Parents and children reading books together. In D. K. Dickinson & P. O. Tabors (Eds.), *Beginning literacy with children: Young children learning at home and school* (pp. 31–51). Baltimore: Brookes.

De Villiers, J. (2003). Defining SLI: A linguistic perspective. In Y. Levy & J. Schaeffer (Eds.), *Language competence across populations: Toward a definition of Specific Language Impairment* (pp. 425–447). Mahwah, NJ: Lawrence Erlbaum Associates.

Dickinson, D. K., & Smith, M. W. (1994). Long-term effects of preschool teachers' book readings on low-income children's vocabulary and story comprehension. *Reading Research Quarterly, 29,* 104–122.

Dillard, J. L. (1972). *Black English: Its history and usage in the United States.* New York: Random House.

Dunn, L. (1959). *Peabody Picture Vocabulary Test.* Circle Pines, MN: American Guidance Service.

Dunn, L., & Dunn, L. (1981). *Peabody Picture Vocabulary Test–Revised.* Circle Pines, MN: American Guidance Service.

Dunn, L., & Dunn, L. (1997). *Peabody Picture Vocabulary Test–III.* Circle Pines, MN: American Guidance Service.

Fasold, R. W. (1972). *Tense marking in Black English.* Washington, DC: Center for Applied Linguistics.

Fasold, R. W., & Wolfram, W. (1970). Some linguistic features of Negro dialect. In R. W. Fasold & R. W. Shuy (Eds.), *Teaching standard English in the inner city, Volume 6* (pp. 41–86). Washington, DC: Center for Applied Linguistics.

Fazio, B., Naremore, R. C., & Connell, P. J. (1996). Tracking children from poverty at risk for specific language impairment: A 3-year longitudinal study. *Journal of Speech and Hearing Research, 39,* 611–624.

Feagans, L., & Haskins, R. (1986). Neighborhood dialogues of Black and White 5-year-olds. *Journal of Applied Developmental Psychology, 7,* 181–200.

Federal Interagency Forum on Child and Family Statistics. (2003). *America's children: Key national indicators of well-being.* (Federal Interagency Forum on Child and Family Statistics). Washington, DC: U.S. Government Printing Office.

Fishback, P. V., & Baskin, J. H. (1991). Narrowing the Black–White gap in child literacy in 1910: The roles of school inputs and family inputs. *The Review of Economics and Statistics, 73,* 725–728.

Fishman, J. A. (1991). *Reversing language shift: Theoretical and empirical foundations of assistance to threatened languages.* New York: Multilingual Matters.

Fletcher, P., & Garman, M. (1988). Normal language development and language impairment: Syntax and beyond. *Clinical Linguistics and Phonetics, 2,* 97–113.

Foorman, B. R., Francis, D. J., Fletcher, J. M., Schatschneider, C., & Mehta, P. (1998). The role of instruction in learning to read: Preventing reading failure in at-risk children. *Journal of Educational Psychology, 90,* 37–55.

Foorman, B. R., & Torgesen, J. (2001). Critical elements of classroom and small-group instruction promote reading success in all children. *Learning Disabilities Research and Practice, 16,* 203–212.

Fordham, S., & Ogbu, J. U. (1996). Black students' school success: Coping with the burden of "acting White." *Urban Review, 18,* 176–206.

Fraser, C., Bellugi, U., & Brown, R. (1963). Control of grammar in imitation, comprehension, and production. *Journal of Verbal Learning and Verbal Behavior, 2,* 121–135.

Fryer, R. G., & Levitt, S. D. (2002). *Understanding the Black–White test score gap in the first two years of school.* Working Paper 8975. Cambridge, MA: National Bureau of Economic Research.

Fudala, J. B. (1974). *Arizona Articulation Proficiency Scale–Revised.* Los Angeles: Western Psychological Services.

Fudala, J. B. (2001). *Arizona Articulation Proficiency Scale* (3rd ed.). Los Angeles: Western Psychological Services.

Fudala, J. B., & Reynolds, W. M. (1986). *Arizona Articulation Proficiency Scale* (2nd ed.). Los Angeles: Western Psychological Services.

Fujiki, M., & Brinton, B. (1987). Elicited imitation revisited: A comparison with spontaneous language production. *Language, Speech, and Hearing Services in Schools, 18,* 301–311.

Gallimore, R., & Goldenberg, C. (2001). Analyzing cultural models and settings to connect minority achievement and school improvement research. *Educational Psychologist, 36*(1), 45–56.

Garmezy, N. (1991). Resilience and vulnerability to adverse developmental outcomes associated with poverty. *American Behavioral Scientist, 34,* 416–430.

Gemake, J. S. (1981). Interference of certain dialect elements with reading comprehension for third graders. *Reading Improvement, 18,* 183–189.

Gill, S., & Reynolds, A. J. (1999). Educational expectations and school achievement of urban African American children. *Journal of School Psychology, 37,* 403–424.

Gleitman, L. R., & Gillette, J. (1999). The role of syntax in verb learning. In W. C. Ritchie & T. K. Bhatia (Eds.), *Handbook of child language acquisition* (pp. 279–295). San Diego, CA: Academic Press.

Golinkoff, R. M., & Hirsh-Pasek, K. (1995). Reinterpreting children's sentence comprehension: Toward a new framework. In P. J. Fletcher & B. MacWhinney (Eds.), *The handbook of child language* (pp. 420–461). Cambridge, MA: Blackwell.

Goldman, R., & Fristoe, M. (1986). *Goldman–Fristoe Test of Articulation.* Circle Pines, MN: American Guidance Service.

Goodman, K. S., & Buck, C. (1973). Dialect barriers to reading comprehension revisited. *The Reading Teacher, 27,* 6–12.

Gopnik, M., & Crago, M. B. (1991). Familial aggregation of a developmental language disorder. *Cognition, 39,* 1–50.

Graham, S. (1994). Motivation in African Americans. *Review of Educational Research, 64,* 55–117.

Gray, S., Plante, E., Vance, R., & Henrichsen, M. (1999). The diagnostic accuracy of four vocabulary tests administered to preschool-age children. *Language, Speech, and Hearing Services in School, 30,* 196–206.

Gray, W. S., & Robinson, H. M. (1967). *Gray Oral Reading Test.* Indianapolis, IN: Bobb-Merrill.

Green, L. J. (1998). Remote past and states in African-American English. *American Speech, 73,* 115–138.

Green, L. J. (2000). Aspectual *be*-type constructions and coercion in African American English. *Natural Language Semantics, 8,* 1–25.

Green, L. J. (2002). *African American English: A linguistic introduction.* Cambridge, England: Cambridge University Press.

Grigg, W. S., Daane, M. C., Jin, Y., & Campbell, J. R. (2003). *The nation's report card: Reading 2002* (NCES 2003-521). Washington, DC: U.S. Department of Education, Institute of Education Sciences, National Center for Education Statistics.

Gutman, L. M., & McLoyd, V. C. (2000). Parents' management of their children's education within the home, at school, and in the community: An examination of African-American families living in poverty. *The Urban Review, 32,* 1–24.

Gutman, L. M., Sameroff, A. J., & Eccles, J. S. (2002). The academic achievement of African American students during early adolescence: An examination of multiple risk, promotive, and protective factors. *American Journal of Community Psychology, 30,* 367–399.

Hammer, C. S. (1999). Guiding language development: How African American mothers and their infants structure play. *Journal of Speech, Language, and Hearing Research, 42,* 1219–1233.

Harber, J. R. (1977). Influence of presentation dialect and orthographic form on reading performance of Black, inner-city children. *Educational Research Quarterly, 2*(2), 9–16.

Harber, J. R. (1982). Accepting dialect renderings of extant materials on Black-English speaking
children's oral reading scores. *Education and Treatment of Children, 5*, 271–282.

Harry, B., & Anderson, M. G. (1994). The disproportionate placement of African American males
in special education programs: A critique of the process. *Journal of Negro Education, 63*,
602–619.

Hart, J. T., Guthrie, J. T., & Winfield, L. (1980). Black English phonology and learning to read. *Journal of Educational Psychology, 72*, 636–646.

Haycock, K., Jerald, C., & Huang, S. (2001). *Closing the gap: Done in a decade.* Washington, DC: Education Trust, Thinking K–16.

Haynes, W. O., & Moran, M. J. (1989). A cross-sectional-developmental study of final consonant
production in southern Black children from preschool through third grade. *Language,
Speech and Hearing Services in Schools, 20*, 400–406.

Headlee Amendment. (1978). Michigan Constitution, Article 9 §§ 6, 25–34.

Heath, S. B. (1983). *Ways with words.* Cambridge, UK: Cambridge University Press.

Hedges, L., & Nowell, A. (1998). Black-White test score convergence since 1965. In C. Jencks & M.
Phillips (Eds.), *The Black-White test score gap* (pp. 149–181). Washington, DC: Brookings Institution Press.

Hester, E. (1996). Narratives of young African American children. In A. Kamhi, K. Pollock, & J.
Harris (Eds.), *Communication development and disorders in African American children* (pp.
227–245). Baltimore: Brookes.

Hinton, L. N., & Pollock, K. E. (2000). Regional variations in the phonological characteristics of African American Vernacular English. *World Englishes, 19*, 39–58.

Hoffer, T. B., Sederstrom, S., Selfa, L., Welch, V., Hess, M., Brown, S., et al. (2003). *Doctorate Recipients from United States Universities: Summary Report 2002.* Chicago: National Opinion Research Center.

Hoffman, K., & Llagas, C. (2003). *Status and trends in the education of Blacks* (NCES 2003-034).
Washington, DC: U.S. Department of Education, National Center for Education Statistics.

Hollingshead, A. B. (1975). *Four factor index of social status.* New Haven, CT: Yale University, Department of Sociology.

Hoover, H. D., Dunbar, S. B., & Frisbie, D. A. (2001). *Iowa Tests of Basic Skills.* Chicago: Riverside
Publishing.

Hunt, K. W. (1970). Syntactic maturity in schoolchildren and adults. *Monographs of the Society for
Research in Child Development, 35*, 1–67. (1, Serial No. 134).

Iceland, J., Weinberg, D. H., & Steinmetz, E. (2002). U.S. Census Bureau, Series CENSR-3, *Racial
and Ethnic Residential Segregation in the United States: 1980–2000.* Washington, DC: U.S. Government Printing Office.

Isaacs, G. J. (1996). Persistence of non-standard dialect in school-age children. *Journal of Speech
and Hearing Research, 3F9*, 434–441.

Jackson, S. C., & Roberts, J. E. (2001). Complex syntax production of African American preschoolers. *Journal of Speech, Language, and Hearing Research, 44*, 1083–1096.

Jencks, C., & Phillips, M. (Eds.). (1998). *The Black-White test score gap.* Washington, DC:
Brookings Institution Press.

Johnson, L. B. (1964). *War on Poverty, President Johnson's 1964 State of the Union Address.* Washington, DC.

Kaufman, A., & Kaufman, N. (1983). *Kaufman Assessment Battery for Children.* Circle Pines, MN:
American Guidance Service.

Klecan-Aker, J. S., & Hedrick, D. L. (1985). A study of the syntactic language skills of normal
school-age children. *Language, Speech, and Hearing Services in Schools, 16*, 187–198.

Klee, T. (1992). Developmental and diagnostic characteristics of quantitative measures of children's language production. *Topics in Language Disorders, 12*(2), 28–41.

Klee, T., & Fitzgerald, M. D. (1985). The relation between grammatical development and mean length of utterance in morphemes. *Journal of Child Language, 12,* 251–269.

Klee, T., Pearce, K., & Carson, D. K. (2000). Improving the positive predictive value of screening for developmental language disorder. *Journal of Speech, Language, and Hearing Research, 43,* 821–833.

Kligman, D., & Cronnell, B. (1974). *Black English and spelling.* Southwest Regional Laboratory for Education Research and Development Technical Report No. 50. Washington, DC: U.S. Department of Health, Education and Welfare. (ERIC Document Reproduction Service No. ED 108 234)

Klima, E. S., & Bellugi, U. (1966). Syntactic regularities in the speech of children. In J. Lyons & R. J. Wales (Eds.), *Psycholinguistics papers* (pp. 183–208). Edinburgh, Scotland: Edinburgh University Press.

Kovac, C. (1980). *Children's acquisition of variable features.* Unpublished doctoral dissertation, Georgetown University, Washington, DC.

Kramer, C., James, S., & Saxman, J. (1979). A comparison of language samples elicited at home and in the clinic. *Journal of Speech and Hearing Disorders, 44,* 321–330.

Labov, W. (1970). *The study of nonstandard English.* Champaign, IL: National Council of Teachers of English.

Labov, W. (1972). *Language in the inner city.* Philadelphia: University of Pennsylvania Press.

Labov, W. (1998). Co-existent systems in African American English. In S. S. Mufwene, J. R. Rickford, G. Bailey, & J. Baugh (Eds.), *African American English: Structure, history, and use* (pp. 110–153). London: Routledge.

Labov, W., Baker, B., Bullock, S., Ross, L., & Brown, M. (1998). *A graphemic-phonemic analysis of the reading errors of inner city children.* Unpublished manuscript. Retrieved June 6, 2001, from http://www.Ling.upenn.edu/~wlabov/Papers/GAREC/GAREC.html

Labov, W., Cohen, P., Robins, C., & Lewis, J. (1968). *A study of the Non-Standard English of Negro and Puerto Rican Speakers in New York City.* Cooperative Research Project No. 3288. Washington, DC: Cooperative Research Program of the Office of Education, U.S. Department of Health, Education and Welfare.

Labov, W., & Harris, W. A. (1986). De facto segregation of black and white vernaculars. In D. Sankoff (Ed.), *Diversity and diachrony* (pp. 1–24). Philadelphia: John Benjamins.

Law, J., Boyle, J., Harris, F., Harkness, A., & Nye, C. (2000). The feasibility of universal screening for primary speech and language delay: Findings from a systematic review of the literature. *Developmental Medicine and Child Neurology, 42,* 190–200.

Lee, L. (1974). *Developmental sentence analysis.* Evanston, IL: Northwestern University Press.

Lee, V. E., & Burkham, D. T. (2002). *Inequality at the starting gate: Social background differences in achievement as children begin school.* Washington, DC: Economic Policy Institute.

Leonard, L. (1972). What is deviant language? *Journal of Speech and Hearing Research, 37,* 427–446.

Leonard, L. B. (1995). Functional categories in the grammars of children with specific language impairment. *Journal of Speech and Hearing Research, 38,* 1270–1283.

Leonard, L. B. (1998). *Children with specific language impairment.* Cambridge, MA: MIT Press.

Loban, W. (1976). *Language development: Kindergarten thru grade twelve.* Urbana, IL: National Council of Teachers.

Loeb, D. F., & Leonard, L. B. (1991). Subject case marking and verb morphology in normally developing and specifically language-impaired children. *Journal of Speech and Hearing Research, 34,* 340–346.

MacWhinney, B. (1994). *The CHILDES project: Tools for analyzing talk* (2nd ed.). Pittsburgh, PA: Carnegie Mellon University.

Manning, M. L., & Baruth, L. G. (2000). *Multicultural education of children and adolescents* (3rd ed.). Boston: Allyn & Bacon.

Maratsos, M., Kuczaj, S., Fox, D., & Chalkley, M. (1979). Some empirical studies in the acquisition of transformational relations: Passives, negatives, and the past tense. In A. Collins (Ed.), *Children's language and communication* (pp. 1–46). Hillsdale, NJ: Lawrence Erlbaum Associates.

Markham, L. R. (1984). "De dog and de cat": Assisting speakers of Black English as they begin to write. *Young Children, 39*(4), 15–24.

Martin Luther King Junior Elementary School Children v. Ann Arbor School District Board. (1979). 463 F. Supp. 1027.

Martin, S., & Wolfram, W. (1998). The sentence in African-American vernacular English. In S. S. Mufwene, J. R. Rickford, G. Bailey, & J. Baugh (Eds.), *African-American English: Structure, history and use* (pp. 11–36). London: Routledge.

McCarthy, D. (1930). The language development of the preschool child. In Y. Brackbill (Ed.), *Infancy and early childhood* (pp. 3–14). New York: The Free Press.

McLoyd, V. C. (1991). What is the study of African American children the study of? In R. L. Jones (Ed.), *Black psychology* (3rd ed., pp. 419–440). Berkeley, CA: Cobb & Henry.

McLoyd, V. C. (1998). Socioeconomic disadvantage and child development. *American Psychologist, 53*, 185–204.

McLoyd, V. C., & Ceballo, R. (1998). Conceptualizing and assessing economic context: Issues in the study of race and child development. In V. C. McLoyd & L. Steinberg (Eds.), *Studying minority adolescents: Conceptual, methodological, and theoretical issues* (pp. 251–278). Mahwah, NJ: Lawrence Erlbaum Associates.

McNeill, D. (1970). *The acquisition of language: The study of developmental psycholinguistics.* New York: Harper & Row.

Melmed, P. J. (1973). Black English phonology: The question of reading interference. In J. L. Laffey & R. W. Shuy (Eds.), *Language differences: Do they interfere?* (pp. 70–85). Newark, DE: International Reading Association.

Menyuk, P. (1964). Syntactic rules used by children from preschool through first grade. *Child Development, 35*, 533–546.

Metropolitan Achievement Tests (7th ed.). (1993). San Antonio, TX: Harcourt Brace.

Michigan Educational Assessment Program, Grade 4. (1999–2001). Lansing, MI: State of Michigan.

Miller, J. F. (1981). *Assessing language production in children: Experimental procedures.* Baltimore: University Park Press.

Miller, J. F. (1991). Quantifying productive language disorders. In J. F. Miller (Ed.), *Research on child language disorders: A decade of progress* (pp. 211–220). Austin, TX: Pro-Ed.

Miller, J. F. (1996). Progress in assessing, describing, and defining child language disorder. In K. N. Cole, P. S. Dale, & D. J. Thal (Eds.), *Assessment of communication and language, Volume 6* (pp. 309–324). Baltimore: Brookes.

Miller, W., & Ervin-Tripp, S. (1964). The development of grammar in child language. In U. Bellugi & R. Brown (Eds.), *The acquisition of language. Monographs of the Society for Research in Child Development* (pp. 9–34). Lafayette, IN: Child Development Publications of the Society for Research in Child Development.

Minority Student Achievement Network. Retrieved September 23, 2004, from http://www.msanetwork.org/aboutus.asp

Morgan, M. (1998). More than a mood or an attitude: Discourse and verbal genres in African-American culture. In S. S. Mufwene, J. R. Rickford, G. Bailey, & J. Baugh (Eds.), *African-American English: Structure, history and use* (pp. 251–281). London: Routledge.

Mufwene, S. S., Rickford, J. R., Bailey, G., & Baugh, J. (Eds.). (1998). *African-American English: Structure, history and use.* London: Routledge.

Nelson, N. W. (1993). *Childhood language disorders in context: Infancy through adolescence.* New York: Macmillan.

Nelson, N. W., & Hyter, Y. D. (1990, November). *How to use Black English Sentence Scoring (BESS) as a tool of non-biased assessment.* Short Course presented at the American Speech-Language-Hearing Association Annual Convention, Seattle, WA.

Nettles, M. T., & Perna, L. W. (1997). *The African American education data book* (Vol. II: Preschool through high school). Ann Arbor, MI: Frederick D. Patterson Research Institute of College Fund/UNCF.

Neuman, S. B., & Roskos, K. (1992). Literacy objects as cultural tools: Effects on children's literacy conversations in play. *Reading Research Quarterly, 27,* 202–225.

Newcomer, P. L., & Hammill, D. D. (1977). *Test of Language Development.* Austin, TX: Pro-Ed.

Ninio, A., & Snow, C. E. (1999). The development of pragmatics: Learning to use language appropriately. In W. C. Ritchie & T. K. Bhatia (Eds.), *Handbook of child language acquisition* (pp. 347–383). San Diego, CA: Academic Press.

No Child Left Behind Act of 2001. (2002). 20 U.S.C. § 6301 et seq.

Oetting, J. B., Cantrell, J. P., & Horohov, J. E. (1999). A study of specific language impairment (SLI) in the context of non-standard dialect. *Clinical Linguistics and Phonetics, 13,* 25–44.

Oetting, J. B., & Cleveland, L. H. (in press). The clinical utility of nonword repetition for children living in the rural South of the US. *Clinical Linguistics and Phonetics.*

Oetting, J. B., & McDonald, J. L. (2001). Nonmainstream dialect use and specific language impairment. *Journal of Speech, Language, and Hearing Research, 44,* 207–223.

Oetting, J. B., & McDonald, J. L. (2002). Methods for characterizing participants' nonmainstream dialect use within studies of child language. *Journal of Speech, Language, and Hearing Research, 45,* 505–518.

Oetting, J. B., & Pruitt, S. (in press). Southern African American English use across groups. *Clinical Linguistics and Phonetics.*

Ogbu, J. U. (1988). Cultural diversity and human development. *New Directions for Child Development, 42,* 11–28.

Ogbu, J. U. (1992). Understanding cultural diversity and learning. *Educational Researcher, 21*(8), 5–14.

Ogbu, J. U. (2003). *Black American students in an affluent suburb: A study of academic disengagement.* Mahwah, NJ: Lawrence Erlbaum Associates.

O'Sullivan, C. Y., Lauko, M. A., Grigg, W. S., Qian, J., & Zhang, J. (2003). *The nation's report card: Science 2000* (NCES 2003-453). Washington, DC: U.S. Department of Education, Institute of Education Sciences, National Center for Education Statistics.

Owens, R. E. (1988). *Language development: An introduction.* Columbus, OH: Merrill.

Owens, R. E., Jr. (2001). *Language development: An introduction* (5th ed.). Boston: Allyn & Bacon.

Owings, W., & Magliaro, S. (1998). Grade retention: A history of failure. *Educational Leadership, 56*(1), 86–88.

Parnell, M. M., Patterson, S. S., & Harding, M. A. (1984). Answers to Wh-questions: A developmental study. *Journal of Speech and Hearing Research, 27,* 297–305.

Patton, J. M. (1998). The disproportionate representation of African Americans in special education: Looking behind the curtain for understanding and solutions. *Journal of Special Education, 32,* 25–31.

Paul, R. (2001). *Language disorders from infancy through adolescence: Assessment and intervention* (2nd ed.). St. Louis, MO: Mosby.

Peisner-Feinberg, E. S., & Burchinal, M. S. (1997). Relations between preschool children's childcare experiences and concurrent development: The cost, quality, and outcomes study. *Merrill-Palmer Quarterly, 43,* 451–477.

Pellegrini, A., Perlmutter, J., Galda, L., & Brody, G. (1990). Joint reading between Black Head Start children and their mothers. *Child Development, 61,* 443–453.

Pendergast, K., Dickey, S., Semlar, J., & Soder, A. (1969). *Photo Articulation Test.* Danville, IL: Interstate Printers.

Perry, T., & Delpit, L. (Eds.). (1998). *The real Ebonics debate: Power, language, and the education of African-American children.* Boston: Beacon Press.

Persky, H. R., Daane, M. C., & Jin, Y. (2003). *The nation's report card: Writing 2002* (NCES 2003-529). Washington, DC: U.S. Department of Education, Institute of Education Sciences, National Center for Education Statistics.

Phillips, M., Brooks-Gunn, J., Duncan, G. J., Klebanov, P., & Crane, J. (1998). Family background, parenting practices, and the Black–White test score gap. In C. Jencks & M. Phillips (Eds.), *The Black–White test score gap* (pp. 103–145). Washington, DC: Brookings Institution Press.

Phillips, M., Crouse, J., & Ralph, J. (1998). Does the Black–White test score gap widen after children enter school? In C. Jencks & M. Phillips (Eds.), *The Black–White test score gap* (pp. 229–272). Washington, DC: Brookings Institution Press.

Piestrup, A. (1973). *Black dialect interference and accommodation of reading instruction in first grade* (Language-Behavior Research Laboratory Monograph No. 4). Berkeley, CA: University of California.

Pike, K. (1967). *Language in relation to a unified theory of the structure of human behavior.* The Hague: Mouton.

Poeppel, D., & Wexler, K. (1993). The full competence hypothesis of clause structure in early German. *Language, 69,* 1–33.

Pollock, K. E., & Berni, M. C. (1997, October). *A phonetic analysis of vocalic and postvocalic /r/ in African American Memphians.* Paper presented at the 25th annual NWAVE (New Ways of Analyzing Variation in English) Conference, Las Vegas, NV.

Portes, O. R. (1996). Ethnicity and culture in educational psychology. In D. C. Berliner & R. C. Calfee (Eds.), *Handbook of educational psychology* (pp. 331–357). New York: Macmillan.

Prutting, C., Gallagher, T., & Mulac, A. (1975). Imitation: A closer look. *Journal of Speech and Hearing Disorders, 41,* 412–422.

Purcell-Gates, V. (1996). Stories, coupons, and the TV Guide: Relationships between home literacy experiences and emergent literacy knowledge. *Reading Research Quarterly, 31,* 406–428.

Ramey, C. T., Campbell, F. A., Burchinal, M., Skinner, M. L., Gardner, D. M., & Ramey, S. L. (2000). Persistent effects of early childhood education on high-risk children and their mothers. *Applied Developmental Science, 4,* 2–14.

Reveron, W. W. (1978). *The acquisition of four Black English morphological rules by Black preschool children.* Unpublished doctoral dissertation, Ohio State University, Columbus.

Rice, M. L. (1998, November). *In search of an inherited grammatical competency.* Paper presented at the ASLHA Annual Meeting, San Antonio, TX.

Rice, M. L. (2000). Grammatical symptoms of specific language impairment. In D. V. M. Bishop & L. B. Leonard (Eds.), *Speech and language impairments in children* (pp. 17–34). Philadelphia: Taylor & Francis.

Rice, M. L. (2003). A unified model of specific and general language delay: Grammatical tense as a clinical marker of unexpected variation. In Y. Levy & J. Schaeffer (Eds.), *Language competence across populations: Toward a definition of Specific Language Impairment* (pp. 63–95). Mahwah, NJ: Lawrence Erlbaum Associates.

Rice, M., & Oetting, J. B. (1993). Morphological deficits of children with SLI: Evaluation of number marking and agreement. *Journal of Speech and Hearing Research, 36,* 1249–1257.

Rice, M., & Wexler, K. (1996). Toward tense as a clinical marker of specific language impairment in English-speaking children. *Journal of Speech and Hearing Research, 39,* 1239–1257.

Rice, M., Wexler, K., & Cleave, P. L. (1995). Specific language impairment as a period of extended optional infinitive. *Journal of Speech and Hearing Research, 38,* 850–863.

Richards, B. (1987). Type/token ratios: What do they really tell us? *Journal of Child Language, 14,* 201–209.

Rickford, J. R. (1997). Prior creolization of African-American vernacular English? Sociohistorical and textual evidence from 17th and 18th centuries. *Journal of Sociolinguistics, 1,* 315–336.

Rickford, J. R. (1998). The Creole origins of African-American vernacular English: Evidence from copula absence. In S. S. Mufwene, J. R. Rickford, G. Bailey, & J. Baugh (Eds.), *African-American English: Structure, history and use* (pp. 154–200). London: Routledge.

Rickford, J. R. (1999). The Ebonics controversy in my backyard: A sociolinguist's experiences and reflections. *Journal of Sociolinguistics, 3,* 267–275.

Rickford, J. R., & Rafal, C. T. (1996). Preterite Had + V-Ed in the narratives of African-American preadolescents. *American Speech, 71,* 227–254.

Roberts, K. (1983). Comprehension and production of word order in Stage I. *Child Development, 54,* 443–449.

Robinson, C. C., Larsen, J. M., & Haupt, J. H. (1996). The influence of selecting and taking picture books home on the at-home reading behaviors of kindergarten children. *Reading Research and Instruction, 35,* 249–259.

Rodekohr, R. K., & Haynes, W. O. (2001). Differentiating dialect from disorder: A comparison of two processing tasks and a standardized language test. *Journal of Communication Disorders, 34,* 255–272.

Ross, S. H., Oetting, J. B., & Stapleton, B. (2004). Preterite *had* + V-*ed*: A developmental narrative structure of African American English. *American Speech, 79,* 167–193.

Russell, A. (1990). The effects of child–staff ratio on staff and child behavior in preschools: An experimental study. *Journal of Research in Childhood Education, 4,* 77–90.

Russo, C. J., & Talbert-Johnson, C. (1997). The over-representation of African American children in special education: The re-segregation of educational programming. *Education and Urban Society, 29,* 136–148.

Rutter, M. (1987). Psychosocial resilience and protective mechanisms. *American Journal of Orthopsychiatry, 57,* 316–331.

Rystrom, R. (1973–1974). Perceptions of vowel letter–sound relationships by first grade children. *Reading Research Quarterly, 2,* 170–185.

Sable, J. (1998). The educational progress of Black students. In J. Wirt, T. Snyder, J. Sable, S. P. Choy, Y. Bae, J. Stennett, A. Gruner, & M. Perie (Eds.), *The condition of education 1998* (NCES 98-013, pp. 2–10). Washington, DC: U.S. Department of Education, National Center for Education Statistics. Retrieved August 14, 2002, from http://nces.ed.gov/pubs98/98013.pdf

Sameroff, A. J., Seifer, R., Barocas, R., Zax, M., & Greenspan, S. (1987). Intelligence quotient scores of 4-year-old children: Social environmental risk factors. *Pediatrics, 79,* 343–350.

Scarborough, H. S. (1998). Early identification of children at risk for reading disabilities: Phonological awareness and some other promising predictors. In B. K. Shapiro, P. J. Accardo, & A. J. Capute (Eds.), *Specific reading disability: A view of the spectrum* (pp. 75–120). Timonium, MD: York Press.

Scarborough, H. S., & Dobrich, W. (1994). On the efficacy of reading to preschoolers. *Developmental Review, 14,* 245–302.

Scarborough, H. S., Wyckoff, J., & Davidson, R. (1986). A reconsideration of the relation between age and mean length of utterance. *Journal of Speech and Hearing Research, 29,* 394–399.

Schepis, M. M., Reid, D. H., Ownbey, J., & Parsons, M. B. (2001). Training support staff to embed teaching within natural routines of young children with disabilities in an inclusive preschool. *Journal of Applied Behavior Analysis, 34,* 313–327.

Scott, C. M. (1988). Spoken and written syntax. In M. A. Nippold (Ed.), *Later language development: Ages nine through nineteen* (pp. 49–95). Boston: College-Hill Press.

Scott, C. M. (2004). Syntactic contributions to literacy learning. In C. A. Stone, E. R. Silliman, B. J. Ehren, & K. Apel (Eds.), *Handbook of language and literacy: Development and disorders* (pp. 340–362). New York: Guilford Press.

Scott, C. M., & Rogers, L. M. (1996). Written language abilities of African American children and youth. In A. G. Kamhi, K. E. Pollock, & J. L. Harris (Eds.), *Communication development and disorders in African American children* (pp. 307–332). Baltimore: Brookes.

Seymour, H. N., Ashton, N., & Wheeler, L. W. (1986). The effect of race on language elicitation. *Language, Speech, and Hearing Services in Schools, 17,* 146–151.

Seymour, H. N., & Ralabate, P. K. (1985). The acquisition of a phonologic feature of Black English. *Journal of Communication Disorders, 18,* 139–148.

Seymour, H. N., & Roeper, T. (1999). Grammatical acquisition of African American English. In O. L. Taylor & L. Leonard (Eds.), *Language acquisition across North America: Cross-cultural and cross-linguistic perspectives* (pp. 109–152). San Diego, CA: Singular Publishing Group.

Seymour, H. N., Roeper, T. W., & de Villiers, J. (2003). *Diagnostic Evaluation of Language Variation.* San Antonio, TX: Psychological Corporation.

Seymour, H. N., & Seymour, C. M. (1981). Black English and Standard American English contrasts in consonantal development of four and five-year old children. *Journal of Speech and Hearing Disorders, 46,* 274–280.

Simons, H. D., & Johnson, K. R. (1973). Black English syntax and reading interference. *Research in the Teaching of English,* 339–358.

Singham, M. (1998). The canary in the mine: The achievement gap between Black and White students. *Phi Delta Kappan, 80,* 8–15.

Singham, M. (2003). The achievement gap: Myths and reality. *Phi Delta Kappan, 84,* 586–591.

Slaughter-Defoe, D. T., & Rubin, H. H. (2001). A longitudinal case study of Head Start eligible children: Implications for urban education. *Educational Psychologist, 36*(1), 31–44.

Smith, M. W., & Dickinson, D. K. (1994). Describing oral language opportunities and environments in Head Start and other preschool classrooms. *Early Childhood Research Quarterly, 9,* 345–366.

Smith, T. T., Bradham, T., Chandler, L., & Wells, D. (2000). The effect of examiner's race on the performance of African-American children on the SCAN. *Language, Speech, and Hearing Services in Schools, 31,* 116–125.

Smitherman, G. (1977). *Talkin and testifyin: The language of Black America.* Boston, MA: Houghton Mifflin.

Smitherman, G. (1998). Word from the hood: The lexicon of African-American Vernacular English. In S. S. Mufwene, J. R. Rickford, G. Bailey, & J. Baugh (Eds.), *African-American English: Structure, history and use* (pp. 203–225). London: Routledge.

Snow, C., Burns, S., & Griffin, M. (Eds.). (1998). *Preventing reading difficulties in young children.* Washington, DC: National Academy Press.

Snow, C. E., & Tabors, P. O. (1993). Language skills that relate to literacy development. In B. Spodek & O. Saracho (Eds.), *Yearbook in early childhood education, Volume 4* (pp. 1–20). New York: Teachers College Press.

Spencer, M. B., Noll, E., Stoltzfus, J., & Harpalani, V. (2001). Identity and school adjustment: Revising the "acting White" assumption. *Educational Psychologist, 36*(1), 21–30.

Standard & Poor's School Evaluation Services. (2002). Data set retrieved September 23, 2004, from http://www.ses.standardandpoors.com

Stark, R., & Tallal, P. (1981). Selection of children with specific language deficits. *Journal of Speech and Hearing Disorders, 46,* 114–122.

Steele, C., & Aronson, J. (1998). Stereotype threat and the test performance of academically successful African Americans. In C. Jencks & M. Phillips (Eds.), *The Black–White test score gap* (pp. 401–430). Washington, DC: Brookings Institution Press.

Steffensen, M. (1974). *The acquisition of Black English.* Unpublished doctoral dissertation, University of Illinois, Evanston.

Steffensen, M. S., Reynolds, R. E., McClure, E., & Guthrie, L. F. (1982). Black English Vernacular and reading comprehension: A cloze study of third, sixth, and ninth graders. *Journal of Reading Behavior, 14,* 285–298.

Stevenson, H. W., Chen, C., & Uttal, D. H. (1990). Beliefs and achievement: A study of Black, White, and Hispanic children. *Child Development, 61,* 508–523.

Stewart, W. A. (1970). Toward a history of American Negro dialect. In F. Williams (Ed.), *Language and poverty: Perspectives on a theme* (pp. 351–379). Chicago: Markham.

Stockman, I. (1984, September). *The development of linguistic norms for nonmainstream populations.* Paper presented at the National Conference on Concerns for Minority Groups in Communication Disorders, Vanderbilt University, Nashville, TN.

Stockman, I. J. (1996). Phonological development and disorders in African American children. In A. G. Kamhi, K. E. Pollock, & J. L. Harris (Eds.), *Communication development and disorders in African American children* (pp. 117–153). Baltimore: Brookes.

Stockman, I. J. (2000). The new Peabody Picture Vocabulary Test–III: An illusion of unbiased assessment? *Language, Speech, and Hearing Services in Schools, 31,* 340–353.

Stockman, I., & Vaughn-Cooke, F. (1982). A re-examination of research on the language of Black children: The need for a new framework. *Journal of Education, 164,* 157–172.

Stockman, I., & Vaughn-Cooke, F. (1984, July). *A closer look at the dynamic and static locative distinctions.* Paper presented at the Third International Child Language Congress, Austin, TX.

Stokes, N. H. (1976). *A cross sectional study of the acquisition of negation structures in Black children.* Unpublished doctoral dissertation, Georgetown University, Washington, DC.

Tager-Flusberg, H. (2001). Putting words together: Morphology and syntax in the preschool years. In J. Berko-Gleason (Ed.), *The development of language* (5th ed., pp. 162–212). Boston: Allyn & Bacon.

Templin, M. C. (1957). *Certain language skills in children: Their development and interrelationships.* Westport, CT: Greenwood.

Templin, M. C., & Darley, F. L. (1969). *Templin–Darley Tests of Articulation* (2nd ed.). Iowa City, IA: University of Iowa Bureau of Education Research and Service.

TerraNova CTBS. (1997). Monterey, CA: CTB/McGraw-Hill.

Terrell, S. L., & Terrell, F. T. (1993). African-American cultures. In D. L. Battle (Ed.), *Communication disorders in multicultural populations* (pp. 3–37). Boston: Andover Medical.

Thomas-Tate, S. R., Washington, J. A., Craig, H. K., & Packard, M. E. W. (2005). *Performances of African American preschool and kindergarten students on the Expressive Vocabulary Test.* Manuscript submitted for publication.

Thompson, C. A. (2003). *The oral vocabulary abilities of skilled and unskilled African American readers.* Unpublished doctoral dissertation, University of Michigan, Ann Arbor.

Thompson, C. A., & Craig, H. K. (2005). *African American students who are proficient or struggling readers: The role of higher order vocabulary abilities.* Manuscript submitted for publication.

Thompson, C. A., Craig, H. K., & Washington, J. A. (2004). Variable production of African American English across oracy and literacy contexts. *Language, Speech, and Hearing Services in Schools, 35,* 269–282.

Toppo, G. (2003, July 2). The face of the American teacher; White and female, while her students are ethnically diverse. *USA Today,* p. D01.

Torgesen, J. K. (1998). Catch them before they fall: Identification and assessment to prevent reading failure in young children. *American Educator, Spring/Summer,* 32–39.

Torgesen, J. K., Wagner, R. K., Rashotte, C. A., Rose, E., Lindamood, P., Conway, T., et al. (1999). Preventing reading failure in young children with phonological processing disabilities: Group and individual responses to instruction. *Journal of Educational Psychology, 91,* 579–593.

Torrey, J. (1972). *The language of Black children in the early grades.* New London: Connecticut College.

Tyack, D., & Ingram, D. (1977). Children's production and comprehension of questions. *Journal of Child Language, 4,* 211–224.

Vellutino, F. R., Scanlon, D. M., Sipay, E. R., Small, S. G., Pratt, A., Chen, R., et al. (1996). Cognitive profiles of difficult to remediate and readily remediated poor readers: Early intervention as a vehicle for distinguishing between cognitive and experiential deficits as basic causes of specific reading disability. *Journal of Educational Psychology, 88,* 601–638.

Vellutino, F. R., Scanlon, D. M., & Tanzman, M. S. (1998). The case for early intervention in diagnosing specific reading disability. *Journal of School Psychology, 36,* 367–397.

Vernon-Feagans, L. (1996). *Children's talk in communities and classrooms.* Cambridge, MA: Blackwell.

Vernon-Feagans, L., Hammer, C. S., Miccio, A., & Manlove, E. (2001). Early language and literacy skills in low-income African American and Hispanic children. In S. B. Neuman & D. K. Dickinson (Eds.), *Handbook of early literacy research* (pp. 192–210). New York: Guilford Press.

Washington, J. A., & Craig, H. K. (1992). Performances of low-income, African American preschool and kindergarten children on the Peabody Picture Vocabulary Test–Revised. *Language, Speech, and Hearing Services in Schools, 23,* 329–333.

Washington, J. A., & Craig, H. K. (1994). Dialectal forms during discourse of urban, African American preschoolers living in poverty. *Journal of Speech and Hearing Research, 37,* 816–823.

Washington, J. A., & Craig, H. K. (1998). Socioeconomic status and gender influences on children's dialectal variations. *Journal of Speech, Language, and Hearing Research, 41,* 618–626.

Washington, J., & Craig, H. (1999). Performances of at-risk, African American preschoolers on the Peabody Picture Vocabulary Test–III. *Language, Speech, and Hearing Services in Schools, 30,* 75–82.

Washington, J. A., & Craig, H. K. (2001). Reading performance and dialectal variation. In J. Harris, A. Kamhi, & K. Pollock (Eds.), *Literacy in African American communities* (pp. 147–168). Mahwah, NJ: Lawrence Erlbaum Associates.

Washington, J. A., & Craig, H. K. (2002). Morphosyntactic forms of African American English used by young children and their caregivers. *Applied Psycholinguistics, 23,* 209–231.

Washington, J. A., & Craig, H. K. (2004). A language screening protocol for use with young African American children in urban settings. *American Journal of Speech-Language Pathology, 13,* 329–340.

Washington, J. A., Craig, H. K., & Kushmaul, A. (1998). Variable use of African American English across two language sampling contexts. *Journal of Speech, Language, and Hearing Research, 41,* 1115–1124.

Wasley, P. A. (2002). Small classes, small schools: The time is now. *Educational Leadership, 59*(5), 6–10.

Watkins, R. V. (1994). Grammatical challenges for children with Specific Language Impairment. In R. V. Watkins & M. L. Rice (Eds.), *Specific Language Impairments in children, Volume 4* (pp. 53–68). Baltimore: Brookes.

Watkins, R. V., Kelly, D. J., Harbers, H. M., & Hollis, W. (1995). Measuring children's lexical diversity: Differentiating typical and impaired language learners. *Journal of Speech and Hearing Research, 38,* 1349–1355.

Weiss, A. R., Lutkus, A. D., Hildebrant, B. S., & Johnson, M. S. (2002). *The nation's report card: Geography 2001* (NCES 2002-484). Washington, DC: U.S. Department of Education, Office of Educational Research and Improvement, National Center for Education Statistics.

Westerlund, M., & Sundelin, C. (2000). Screening for developmental language disability in 3-year-old children. Experiences from a field study in a Swedish municipality. *Child: Care, Health, and Development, 26,* 91–110.

Whitehurst, G. J., Epstein, J. N., Angell, A. L., Payne, A. C., Crone, D. A., & Fischel, J. E. (1994). Outcomes of emergent literacy intervention in Head Start. *Journal of Educational Psychology, 86,* 542–555.

Whitehurst, G. J., & Lonigan, C. L. (2001). Emergent literacy: Development from prereaders to readers. In S. B. Neuman & D. K. Dickinson (Eds.), *Handbook of early literacy research* (pp. 11–29). New York: Guilford Press.

Wiederholt, J. L., & Bryant, B. R. (1992). *Gray Oral Reading Tests, Third Edition.* Austin, TX: Pro-Ed.

Wiederholt, J. L., & Bryant, B. R. (2001). *Gray Oral Reading Tests, Fourth Edition.* Austin, TX: Pro-Ed.

Wiener, F. D., Lewnau, L. E., & Erway, E. (1983). Measuring language competency in speakers of Black American English. *Journal of Speech and Hearing Disorders, 48,* 76–84.

Williams, K. (1997). *Expressive Vocabulary Test.* Circle Pines, MN: American Guidance Service.

Williams, K., & Wang, Y. (1997). *Technical manual: Peabody Picture Vocabulary Test–III.* Circle Pines, MN: American Guidance Service.

Willig, A. C., Harnisch, D. L., Hill, K. T., & Maehr, M. L. (1983). Sociocultural and educational correlates of success–failure attributions and evaluation anxiety in the school setting for Black, Hispanic, and Anglo children. *American Educational Research Journal, 20,* 385–410.

Winford, D. (1997). On the origins of African American Vernacular English: A Creolist perspective. *Diachronica, 14,* 305–344.

Wolfram, W. (1971). Black and white speech differences revisited. In W. Wolfram & N. Clarke (Eds.), *Black–White speech relationships* (pp. 139–161). Washington, DC: Center for Applied Linguistics.

Wolfram, W. (1994). The phonology of a sociocultural variety: The case of African American Vernacular English. In J. Bernthal & N. Bankston (Eds.), *Child phonology: Characteristics, assessment and intervention with special populations* (pp. 227–244). New York: Thieme.

Wolfram, W., Adger, C. T., & Christian, D. (1999). *Dialects in schools and communities.* Mahwah, NJ: Lawrence Erlbaum Associates.

Wolfram, W., & Fasold, R. (1974). *The study of social dialects in American English.* Englewood Cliffs, NJ: Prentice Hall.

Wolfram, W., & Schilling-Estes, N. (1998). *American English: Dialects and variation.* Malden, MA: Blackwell.

Wong, C. A., & Rowley, S. J. (2001). The schooling of ethnic minority children: Commentary. *Educational Psychologist, 36*(1), 57–66.

Woodcock, R. W. (1987). *Woodcock Reading Mastery Tests, Revised.* Circle Pines, MN: American Guidance Service.

Wyatt, T. A. (1996). Acquisition of the African American English copula. In A. G. Kamhi, K. E. Pollock, & J. L. Harris (Eds.), *Communication development and disorders in African American children: Research, assessment, and intervention* (pp. 95–115). Baltimore: Brookes.

Author Index

SUBJECT INDEX

A

African American English
dialect density measure (DDM), 1, 43–51
  community and, 49–50
  context and, 50–51
  grade and, 45–48
  socioeconomic status, gender and,
    48–49, 130–131
dialect shifting, 45–48, 98–100
distributional properties, 40–43
features
  checklist, 150
  contrastive and noncontrastive, 10
  developmental patterns and, 29–30
  language impairments and, 33–35, 72
  low prestige, 38–39
  morpho-syntactic, 35–37, 119–126
  phonological, 37–38, 126–129
  uniqueness of, 26
reading and, 95–100
research perspectives, 8–12
  etic–emic approach, 31–35
  nondiscriminatory language evaluation,
    12
  sociolinguistic, 11–12
  Universal Grammar, 8–11
terminology
  African American Vernacular English, 28
  Black English, 28
  Ebonics, 28

Southern African American English, 27,
  73
writing and, 102–106
African American Vernacular English, see
  African American English
Ann Arbor Decision, 5–6, 107
Arizona Articulation Proficiency Scale, 27,
  64, 69, 72

B

Black English, see African American English
Black English case, see Ann Arbor Decision
Black–White Achievement Gap
  classroom environments and attitudes to
    schooling and, 87–92
  early family literacy practices and, 92–93
  future directions, 93–94
  poverty and, 83–87
  test score differences, 5–6, 16–17, 81,
    109–110
Black–White Test Score Gap, see
  Black–White Achievement Gap
Brown v. Board of Education, 5, 107

C

Clinical Evaluation of Language
  Fundamentals (CELF), 69